Dao & Zen

Dan Olman

Dao & Zen

Copyright © 2025 Dan Olman
All rights reserved.

Thank you for buying an authorized edition of this book and for complying with copyright laws against reproduction, distribution, or transmission in any form or by any means, electronic, mechanical, photocopying, recording, or otherwise

---

While every effort has been made to ensure accuracy, the author and publisher assume no responsibility for errors or omissions, or for any consequences arising from the use of information contained in this book.

ISBN: 978-1-0697667-1-7
Presse Arche Vérité
Canada
First Edition, 2025

Printed in the United States of America

Table of Contents

Chapter 1: Zhou Era Philosophy   1
  A Historical Overview
  A Legacy of Dialectical Thought
  The Way of Confucius (Kongzi)
  Mozi: The Philosopher of Universal Love
  Shang Yang and the Legalist School

Chapter 2: Dao: The Way of the Mystics   22
  Mythical Foundations
  Laozi: The Old Master
  Zhuangzi: Literary Genius
  Philosophical Tenets of Daoism

Chapter 3: YIN-YANG: The Cosmic Polarity   43
  Pre-Systematic Origins
  Defining Yin and Yang
  The Integration of Yin-Yang into Daoism
  A Harmonious World View

Chapter 4: The Arrival of Buddhism   59
  Cultural Context of Transmission
  Chan Buddhism – Dao Meets Dharma

Chapter 5: Inner Alchemy and Martial Arts   74
  Neidan: Inner Alchemy
  Chinese Martial Arts
  Tai Chi Chuan: The Supreme Ultimate Fist

Chapter 6: Zen: The Eastward Journey of Dao   92
  The Transmission of Chan to Japan
  Zen's Arrival in Japan: The Kamakura Period
  The Heart of Zen: A Philosophy of Direct Experience

Chapter 7: Epilogue – The Way Beyond Words   108

Introduction

In the vast landscape of human thought, few traditions have offered such profound insights into the nature of existence, perception, and harmony as the Daoist and Zen philosophies. Born from the fertile intellectual soil of Zhou Dynasty China, Daoism (道家) emerged as a mystical response to the turbulence of competing political and ethical systems. While Confucianism sought to reform society through moral cultivation and structured governance, Daoism arose as a gentle rebellion—not imposing new structures, but awakening individuals to the deeper rhythms of the cosmos itself.

Zen (禪), its spiritual descendant, flowered centuries later as Buddhism encountered this Daoist sensibility. What emerged was neither purely Indian nor Chinese, but something entirely new: a path of lived mystical experience that preserved the paradoxical wisdom of both traditions while reaching beyond their limitations.

This book invites you on a contemplative journey through these interconnected streams of wisdom—not merely as an academic survey, but as a meditation on the living pulse that animates both Dao and Zen. We begin in the intellectual crucible of the Zhou era, where the "Hundred Schools of Thought" competed for the soul of Chinese civilization. Against this backdrop of Confucian moralism, Mohist utilitarianism, and Legalist authoritarianism, the Daoist sages Laozi and Zhuangzi emerge as unlikely revolutionaries—mystic guides who led seekers not toward answers, but into the fertile darkness of questions that dissolve themselves.

Rather than treating these traditions as timeless abstractions floating above history, we situate them within the dynamic currents of cultural transmission and transformation. We trace how Daoist insights were preserved, challenged, and reinterpreted across centuries—evolving from philosophical speculation into popular religion, from mystical poetry into alchemical practice, from Chinese wisdom into Japanese art.

Our exploration unfolds through several interconnected movements. We examine the mythical and historical foundations of Daoism, unpacking the textual treasures of the *Dao De Jing* and *Zhuangzi* while illuminating their core insights: *wu wei* (effortless action), *ziran* (spontaneous naturalness), and the ineffable mystery of Dao itself. We witness Daoism's remarkable metamorphosis from elite philosophy into a living religious tradition embracing inner alchemy (*neidan*), ritual practice, and cosmic speculation.

The metaphysical framework of Yin and Yang receives careful attention—not as exotic Eastern symbols, but as sophisticated tools for understanding dynamic relationship and complementary opposition. Beginning with their pre-systematic appearance in the *I Ching* and early agricultural observations, we follow their formal integration into Daoist cosmology, traditional medicine, and the understanding of both natural and social orders.

Our journey continues eastward as Buddhism encountered Chinese soil, giving birth to Chan—a revolutionary synthesis of Indian meditative rigor with Daoist spontaneity and paradox. We explore how Buddhist concepts like emptiness (*śūnyatā*), karma, and rebirth were transformed through their encounter with existing Daoist and Confucian worldviews, creating something unprecedented in the history of contemplative practice.

The embodied dimensions of these teachings receive their due through examination of martial arts and energy cultivation. Tai Chi and Qigong emerge not as mere physical exercises but as moving meditations grounded in Daoist physiology and cosmology—practices where the refinement of the body mirrors the greater cosmic dance of transformation.

Following Chan's migration to Japan, we witness its flowering into Zen, with its distinctive emphasis on direct experience over scriptural authority, its integration into samurai culture, and its aesthetic refinement of the Daoist appreciation for spontaneity and paradox. Here the tradition reveals new facets while preserving its essential spirit.

What emerges through this historical and comparative lens is not a unified dogma but a way of being—flexible yet grounded, simple yet profound, free from artifice yet responsive to circumstance. From the inward laboratories of Daoist alchemy to the wordless transmissions between Zen masters, these traditions offer not conclusions but invitations to participate in the ineffable flow of existence.

Throughout this exploration, we resist the temptation toward essentialism, instead highlighting the historical contingency and philosophical development that shaped these living traditions. Dao and Zen appear not as static doctrines but as creative responses to recurring human crises—always negotiating between inner and outer, mystical and practical, immediate and eternal.

The ongoing dialectic between word and silence, structure and spontaneity, form and emptiness offers a meditation on the elusive nature of the Way (Dao) as it continues to inspire both scholars and practitioners across cultures and centuries. In this spirit, the book addresses both specialist and seeker, inviting consideration not only of what these traditions have taught, but of what they have accomplished: how they have shaped lives, cultures, and fundamental conceptions of reality across millennia.

Whether you approach as philosopher or practitioner, student of religion or martial artist, this book offers pathways into the silence between words, the insight behind paradox, and the way that, in its very essence, cannot be captured in any name we might give it.

Chapter 1

Zhou Era Philosophy

A Historical Overview

The Zhou era, spanning roughly from 1046 to 256 BCE, was a time of immense intellectual ferment in ancient China—a period in which philosophy emerged as a vital force for ordering society, understanding the cosmos, and guiding human conduct. Central to this philosophical flowering was the inheritance of a rich literary tradition, most notably *The Book of Odes* (*Shijing*), an anthology of poetry said to have been compiled or edited by Confucius himself. This text provided the earliest Chinese philosophers with a mirror of culture, emotion, and history through which they could reflect on their own society [1].

The Literary Foundation of Zhou Philosophy

The Book of Odes served as a cornerstone for philosophical reflection during the Zhou era. Comprising poems from the preceding Shang dynasty and from the early Zhou period, it included everything from love songs of striking sensitivity to verses that subtly criticized or praised political events and conditions [2]. For thinkers like Confucius, these texts were not merely literary; they were ethical and historical documents—evidence of human feeling and judgment through time. They allowed reflection upon change and continuity, justice and corruption, and the joys and sufferings of the common people. With this written heritage, the Zhou sages could engage in a dialogue across generations, forming opinions not in isolation but in relation to a recognizable, shared past.

The philosophical texts of the Zhou era were not transmitted in fixed form but evolved through oral recitation, mnemonic devices, and inscription on perishable materials such as bamboo and silk. Many were compiled centuries later, often under imperial patronage, and canonized through editorial processes that reflected shifting political and metaphysical priorities. This layered transmission history underscores both the fragility of the sources and the reverence accorded to them, as each generation reinterpreted inherited wisdom through its own lens of ritual, governance, and cosmology [3].

Against this backdrop of literary and historical consciousness arose the famed "Hundred Schools of Thought," a term used to describe the competing philosophies of the Eastern Zhou period, particularly during its Spring and Autumn (770–476 BCE) and Warring States (475–221 BCE) phases [4]. As the Zhou dynasty's political cohesion declined and regional warlords vied for supremacy, intellectuals were both inspired and compelled to offer visions of order and morality. These visions would become the foundation of Chinese metaphysics, ethics, and political theory for millennia.

Confucianism

Confucius (Kongzi, 551–479 BCE), perhaps the most influential Zhou philosopher, drew heavily on the historical and poetic texts of the past, such as *The Book of Odes* and *The Book of Documents*, to construct a moral philosophy rooted in ritual propriety (*li*), humaneness (*ren*), and the cultivation of virtuous character [5]. He believed the past held the keys to ethical clarity and social harmony. Confucius viewed the moral order as something that could be restored by emulating the sage-kings of antiquity and aligning personal conduct with the rhythms of Heaven (*Tian*).

Daoism

Contrasting sharply with the Confucian emphasis on structure and ritual, Laozi, the semi-legendary author of the *Dao De Jing* (*Tao Te Ching*), offered a mystical and metaphysical alternative: the Dao (Tao), or the ineffable Way, which underlies all things [6]. While also influenced by early traditions like *The Book of Odes*, Daoist thinkers turned reflection inward and emphasized spontaneity (*ziran*), non-action (*wu wei*), and harmony with the natural flow of the cosmos. For Laozi and the Daoist philosophers, the elaborate structures of Confucian morality were seen as artificial interference in the simplicity and profundity of the natural order.

Mohism

Another major figure of the Zhou philosophical landscape was Mozi (c. 470–391 BCE), who reacted against the family-centered ethics of Confucius with a doctrine of *jian ai*, or impartial, universal love. Drawing from logical reasoning and a proto-utilitarian ethical framework, Mozi advocated meritocracy, pacifism, and communal care as means to bring order to the fractured world of the Warring States. His school prized frugality, discipline, and scientific observation, foreshadowing elements of later rationalist thought. The Mohists were also known for their expertise in defensive warfare and logic, developing sophisticated arguments to defend their positions [7].

The Confucian Legacy

Confucius's legacy was further developed by Mencius (Mengzi, 372–289 BCE) and Xunzi (c. 310–235 BCE), two towering figures who debated the fundamental nature of human beings. Mencius claimed that human nature was inherently good, like a seed yearning to sprout, needing only nurturing conditions to flourish [8]. He developed the concept of the "four beginnings" (*si duan*)—innate moral tendencies that, when cultivated, develop into the virtues of benevolence, righteousness, propriety, and wisdom.

Xunzi, by contrast, argued that human nature was selfish and brutish, and that only through rigorous education, laws, and ritual discipline could virtue be cultivated [9]. Despite their opposing views on human nature, both thinkers were deeply steeped in the texts of earlier ages, especially *The Book of Odes*, which offered case studies of human emotion, societal rise and fall, and moral striving.

Legalism

Another major school, Legalism (Fa Jia), emerged with thinkers such as Han Feizi (c. 280–233 BCE), who took a more austere, pragmatic stance on governance. Legalists viewed morality and education as unreliable tools for ruling and instead emphasized strict laws (*fa*), administrative techniques (*shu*), and positional power (*shi*).

While not dismissive of the historical record, they were skeptical of relying on tradition and sentiment, focusing instead on maintaining state power and social order in a time of political chaos. The Legalist philosophy would eventually provide the theoretical foundation for the Qin dynasty's unification of China in 221 BCE, though its harsh implementation led to that dynasty's rapid collapse.

A Legacy of Dialectical Thought

The philosophers of the Zhou era engaged not merely in isolated speculation but in a continuous, critical dialogue. They read and responded to one another, referencing shared texts and historical moments. Through this dialectical process—often in direct debate—they developed a uniquely Chinese philosophical tradition that balanced metaphysics and ethics, pragmatism and mysticism, hierarchy and spontaneity [6].

Beyond the major schools described above, the Zhou period also saw the development of the School of Names (Ming Jia), which explored language and logic, and the Yin-Yang School, which developed a cosmological system based on the interaction of complementary forces in nature. This latter approach would significantly influence Chinese medicine, divination, and natural philosophy for centuries to come [10].

Thus, during the Zhou there were a constellation of philosophical schools whose views competed for influence among the Chinese polity of the times, and which would echo through Chinese civilization for millennia. Anchored in the poetic and historical traditions of *The Book of Odes* and other works, these schools transformed ancient reflections into systematic worldviews, grappling with the deepest questions of human life, social harmony, and cosmic order.

The Confucians looked to the past for order and stability, believing that virtue (*ren*) and ritual (*li*) could restore social harmony, while Daoists withdrew from the artificial institutions of society, trusting in the Dao to harmonize all things through non-action and naturality. The Mohists were utilitarian reformers, opposed to Confucius' emphasis on rituals and proposing universal love as the key to social harmony. The Legalists were a school of political realists, seeing law and order as the only viable tools in an age of chaos.

While these opposing forces vied for dominance in the hearts and minds of the people, the Yin-Yang cosmology arose offering a metaphysical synthesis, interpreting nature and society as governed by dynamic polarities and cyclical processes. This rich philosophical heritage would continue to evolve throughout Chinese history, influencing not just intellectual discourse but art, literature, governance, and daily life across East Asia.

Of the schools we've discussed, the Confucius school and the Daoist schools became the most influential, although many of the others had impact on these two. Some were reactionary, some were syncretic. Next we will discuss the relationships of these schools with each other, and then we'll discuss each school separately.

Following are the major schools of Chinese thought during the Zhou era, showing some of their characteristics.

Thinker	Key Texts	Method of Cultivation	Metaphysical Orientation	Social Order
Confucius	*Analects, Book of Odes, Book of Documents*	Cultivation through ritual (*li*), learning, filial piety	Humanity innately good or perfectible (esp. Mencius) *Ren* (benevolence), *Li* (ritual), *Junzi* (noble person)	Hierarchical meritocracy led by virtuous rulers (*junzi*). Heaven (*Tian*) as moral force, tradition as order.
Daoism (Taoism)	*Dao Te Ching, Zhuangzi*	Non-action (*wu wei*), returning to simplicity	Hamanity neither good nor bad; natural and spontaneous *Dao* as the ineffable origin of all things *Wu wei, Ziran* (naturalness), *Dao* (Way)	Minimal government, harmony through non-interference

Thinker	Key Texts	Method of Cultivation	Metaphysical Orientation	Social Order
Mohism	*Mozi*	Logical argument, utility, universal moral education	Humanity as morally neutral; shaped by education and society. Practical ethics, *Jian ai* (universal love), utilitarianism, frugality	Meritocratic and pacifist, anti-ritual
Legalism	*Han Feizi*, *The Book of Lord Shang*	Law, coercion, strict discipline	Humanity as selfish, shortsighted, pleasure-seeking. *Fa* (law), *Shu* (method), *Shi* (power)	Strong centralized state, clear laws and punishments
Mencius (Mengzi)	*Mencius*	Moral intuition, nurturing environment	Humanity innately good (like sprouts) Four Beginnings (*ce xin*), moral development.	Ruler as moral exemplar; education as foundation. Heaven endows moral nature, mandate of Heaven.
Xunzi	*Xunzi*	Rational education, ritual training	Humanity inherently selfish or evil. Human order creates meaning; no natural moral Heaven	Authoritarian but moral rule; strong institutions. *Li* as social invention, transformation of nature

Thinker	Key Texts	Method of Cultivation	Metaphysical Orientation	Social Order
Yin-Yang & Five Elements	*Guanzi*, *Huainanzi*	Alignment with natural cycles	Part of cosmic balance. Cosmological dualism: Yin-Yang, Wu Xing. Cyclic cosmology, natural philosophy	Rule in harmony with Heaven's rhythms

Relationships between philosophical schools

The various philosophical schools that emerged during the Zhou Dynasty (particularly the Warring States period, 475-221 BCE) developed in conversation with one another, creating a rich intellectual ecosystem where ideas were debated, borrowed, and transformed.

The relationship between Confucianism and Daoism represents perhaps the most important philosophical dialectic in Chinese intellectual history. They existed in complementary opposition; Confucianism focused on social order and ritual propriety, while Daoism emphasized naturalness and spontaneity. Despite their differences, they came to be seen as complementary rather than contradictory approaches to life.

The writings of Zhuangzi frequently satirized Confucian ritual-obsession and artificiality. Laozi criticized the Confucian emphasis on moral cultivation as unnatural [6]. These critiques forced Confucians to refine their positions. By the Song dynasty (960-1279 CE), Neo-Confucians like Zhu Xi incorporated Daoist cosmological concepts, creating a more metaphysically robust Confucianism.
Confucian Development

The two major Confucian thinkers Mencius and Xunzi developed opposing views of human nature. Mencius argued that humans are innately good, while Xunzi claimed human nature is evil and must be corrected through ritual and education. This internal debate enriched Confucian understanding of moral psychology. Xunzi's emphasis on ritual as a controlling mechanism and his skepticism about human nature influenced his student Han Feizi, who would become a founder of Legalism.

Daoist Diversification

The philosophical Daoism of Laozi and Zhuangzi eventually gave rise to a religious Daoism wove together folk religion, celestial-master movements, and yin-yang cosmology. By the late Zhou and early Han periods, interest in longevity (*yangsheng*) and the quest for immortality (*xian*) merged with Daoist philosophy, shifting its focus from sage-king wisdom to practical techniques of body and spirit cultivation [11].

During the Han Dynasty, Daoist thought became increasingly integrated with Yin-Yang cosmology and Five Elements theory, producing a comprehensive natural philosophy that explained seasonal change, disease, and dynastic cycles as manifestations of cosmic resonance [12].

Beginning in the Eastern Han, new texts claiming divine revelation appeared, such as the *Taiping Jing* (Scripture of Great Peace), presenting themselves as authentic transmissions from celestial beings. Zhang Daoling founded the Celestial Master movement in 142 CE, claiming to receive revelations from Laozi, deified as Lord Lao. He established an ecclesiastical structure with priests, rituals for healing, and moral codes. that blended Daoist concepts with elements of Confucian ethics.

Local gods, ancestor worship, and popular religious practices were absorbed into Daoist frameworks, with Daoist priests often taking on roles similar to shamans in mediating between the human and spirit worlds. As Buddhism entered China, Daoism borrowed concepts like karma, rebirth, and monastic organization, while positioning itself as the indigenous alternative to the foreign religion.

Two major alchemical paths developed within religious Daoism. The practices of external alchemy (*waidan*) were focused on achieve immortality through mineral elixirs and herbs. Internal alchemy (*neidan*) emphasized meditative practices to cultivate and refine vital energies within the body [11].

Philosophical Daoism maintained interest among educated elites who were often skeptical of religious practices, while religious Daoism was more popular with the masses, although many scholar-officials did participate in religious Daoist rituals.

Mohism as Catalyst

Mohism directly challenged Confucian emphasis on family-based morality with its concept of universal love. This forced Confucians like Mencius to develop more sophisticated defenses of their hierarchical ethics. Mohist logical argumentation influenced later philosophical discourse across schools [7].

Legalism's Pragmatic Synthesis

Legalists adopted Confucian emphasis on order and Daoist insights about natural principles, but rejected their moral foundations in favor of pragmatic statecraft. While Legalism's explicit philosophy fell from favor after the Qin dynasty's fall, its institutional innovations were incorporated into imperial governance under a Confucian veneer.

Yin-Yang School: Metaphysical Foundation

The correlative cosmology of the Yin-Yang school provided metaphysical underpinnings eventually embraced by nearly all other schools [12]. This cosmological system became integrated into both Confucian and Daoist thought, providing a framework for understanding seasonal changes, dynastic cycles, and human physiology.

By the Han Dynasty, philosophical boundaries blurred as the imperial state adopted Confucianism as its official ideology while incorporating elements from other schools.
The Han synthesis maintained Confucian ritual and ethics while employing Legalist administrative techniques, and Yin-Yang and Five Elements theories became incorporated into mainstream Confucian thought.

Daoism continued as an alternative philosophical perspective, especially for scholars disillusioned with political life. This dynamic interplay between competing yet mutually influencing philosophical traditions created China's distinct intellectual landscape, characterized by pragmatic synthesis rather than strict adherence to a philosophical system.

Let's look at some of these schools in more detail:

The Way of Confucius (Kongzi)

Confucius (551–479 BCE), known in Chinese as Kong Qiu or Kong Fuzi (Master Kong), was born in the small state of Lu in what is now Shandong province. His family, though once noble, had fallen on difficult times, and he grew up in relative poverty. His father died when Confucius was only three years old, leaving his mother to raise him in humble circumstances. This experience of downward social mobility would later inform his deep concern with social order and stability [1].

As a young man, Confucius held minor government positions, including roles as a keeper of granaries and supervisor of public fields. These modest beginnings gave him firsthand insight into the practical challenges of governance and the lives of common people. Unlike many philosophers who spoke from positions of privilege, Confucius's teachings were grounded in lived experience and practical concerns [6].

Confucius lived during a time of political fragmentation and declining ritual order. The Zhou kings had become mere figureheads, and regional warlords competed ruthlessly for power. The ancient system of ritual and music that had once unified Chinese civilization was crumbling. In this turbulent environment, Confucius sought not innovation, but a return to the moral order of a mythic past. His great project was to revive the ancient rites (*li*), restore propriety, and cultivate a moral elite who would rule through virtue (*de*) rather than coercion [5].

"The Master said, 'When the rites are lost, seek them in the countryside.'" — *Analects* 10.27

This famous saying reflects his belief that authentic traditions were often better preserved among common people than at corrupt courts. Throughout his life, Confucius traveled extensively between various states, seeking a ruler who would implement his ideas. Despite his eloquence and wisdom, he largely failed to find lasting political patronage—a source of profound disappointment to him. Instead, his greatest achievement became his role as a teacher, gathering disciples who preserved and transmitted his wisdom.

Educational Mission

Confucius revolutionized education in ancient China by accepting students regardless of their social background—focusing on merit rather than hereditary privilege. He is traditionally credited with teaching around seventy-two disciples, though the number varies in different accounts. His school became the first significant private educational institution in Chinese history, creating a model that would influence educational practices for millennia.

He saw human beings as perfectible through education and ritual, believing that ethical behavior arose not from nature alone, but from discipline, modeling, and reverence for tradition. This optimistic view of human potential contrasts sharply with some Western philosophical traditions that emphasize inherent human flaws or original sin.

"By nature, men are nearly alike; by practice, they get to be wide apart." — *Analects* 17.2

Confucius's teaching method emphasized dialogue, questioning, and practical application rather than mere memorization. The *Analects*, compiled by his disciples after his death, preserves fragments of these conversations, revealing his skill at adapting his instruction to each student's character and needs.

Central Tenets

Confucius's philosophical system rests on several interconnected concepts that form the foundation of his ethical and political thought:

Ren (仁) – Benevolence or human-heartedness.

"The man of ren wishes to establish himself; he helps others to establish themselves. He wishes to develop himself; he helps others to develop." — *Analects* 6.30

Ren begins with filial piety and family reverence but extends outward to embrace all human relationships. It represents not just kindness but a profound recognition of our interconnectedness as human beings.

Li (礼) – Ritual propriety; the system of ritual practices, etiquette, and social customs.

"Without li, respectfulness becomes laborious bustle; carefulness becomes timidity; boldness becomes insubordination; straightforwardness becomes rudeness." — *Analects* 8.2

Li provides the forms through which we express our moral intentions. By observing appropriate ritual behavior, individuals internalize ethical principles and cultivate virtue. The precise performance of ritual creates not just external order but internal moral development.

Junzi (君子) – The noble person, cultivated through moral effort.

"The junzi concerns himself with righteousness; the small man concerns himself with profit." — *Analects* 4.16

The junzi cultivates internal virtues while maintaining appropriate external conduct. Key characteristics include moral integrity, ritual propriety, filial piety, loyalty, and continuous self-improvement. The junzi serves as both a moral exemplar and a fit leader for society.

Zhengming (正名) – Rectification of names; encompasses social roles and conduct.

"If names are not correct, language will not be in accordance with the truth of things. If language is not in accordance with the truth of things, affairs cannot be carried on to success." — *Analects* 13.3

For society to function properly, rulers must rule as true rulers should, fathers must fulfill their proper responsibilities as fathers, and so on. This principle extends to all social relationships and institutions, ensuring that reality matches ideals.

Tian (天) – Heaven, not as a deity, but as a moral ordering principle.

"He who offends against Heaven has none to whom he can pray." — *Analects* 3.13

Heaven bestows the "Mandate of Heaven" (*tianming*) on virtuous rulers and withdraws it from corrupt ones. Confucius saw himself as working in harmony with Heaven's will, though he focused primarily on human affairs rather than metaphysical speculation. He transformed the concept of *Tian* (Heaven) from a personal deity into a more abstract moral force that orders the cosmos.

Relational Ethics

At the heart of Confucian ethics is a vision of human life as fundamentally relational. Individuals exist not in isolation but within a network of "five relationships" (*wulun*):

Ruler and subject (righteousness and loyalty)
Father and son (loving kindness and filial piety)
Husband and wife (distinction in roles and mutual respect)
Elder and younger (proper order and respect for elders)
Friend and friend (trustworthiness and sincerity)

Each relationship entails reciprocal duties and virtues. Even the hierarchical relationships are not merely about obedience but about mutual obligation—a ruler must be benevolent to merit loyalty; parents must be loving to deserve filial piety.

"The Master said: 'In serving your father and mother, remonstrate with them gently. If you see that they are not inclined to follow your advice, remain respectful and do not antagonize them. Though tired, do not complain.'" — *Analects* 4.18

This vision of society as a web of properly conducted relationships stands in contrast to both individualism and strict authoritarianism. It presents a communitarian ethic where self-cultivation always occurs within social contexts.

Legacy

Confucius died in 479 BCE, disappointed that his political vision had not been implemented in his lifetime. However, his disciples preserved his teachings, and within a few centuries, Confucianism would become the dominant philosophical system in China.

The Han dynasty (206 BCE–220 CE) eventually adopted Confucianism as state orthodoxy, establishing the imperial examination system based on Confucian classics [3]. This system would shape Chinese government and society for two millennia, creating a meritocratic ideal of government by scholar-officials immersed in Confucian learning.

Confucius's emphasis on education, moral self-cultivation, family reverence, and social harmony continues to influence East Asian cultures today. His philosophical legacy stands as one of the most enduring systems of ethical thought in human history—a testament to his insight into the foundations of human flourishing and social order.

Mozi: The Philosopher of Universal Love

Amidst this chaos of competing states and ideologies, Mozi (墨子, c. 470-391 BCE) emerged as one of China's most distinctive philosophical voices. Born approximately a century after Confucius, Mozi emerged from humble origins, possibly as a craftsman or minor military official—a background that significantly shaped his worldview. Mozi developed a philosophy that stood in stark contrast to Confucian tradition.

While Confucianism emphasized hierarchy and ritual, Mozi championed meritocracy, practicality, and universal moral concern. He established a highly organized group of followers who not only taught his doctrines but actively intervened in conflicts. Traveling to war-torn regions, they offered their services as diplomatic envoys and military defense consultants, often at great personal risk, in order to prevent bloodshed. They were known for their expertise in defensive warfare, engineering, and logic—practical skills that complemented their ethical teachings [7].

Unlike the aristocratic foundations of Confucianism, Mozi's lowly social status gave him intimate familiarity with the struggles of common people. He witnessed firsthand how war and extravagance among the ruling classes devastated ordinary citizens, observations that would form the cornerstone of his philosophical system.

At the heart of Mozi's philosophy was the revolutionary concept of "Jian Ai" (兼愛) or Universal Love. He argued that social chaos and warfare stemmed from partiality—from people favoring their own families, clans, and states over others. "If people regarded others' states as they regard their own," he reasoned, "who would raise up armies and make war?" This principle directly challenged the Confucian emphasis on filial piety and hierarchical social relationships [6].

Unlike the Daoists who viewed Heaven as an impersonal force, Mozi spoke of "Tian" (Heaven) almost theistically—as a conscious, moral entity that actively rewards good and punishes evil. "Heaven desires righteousness and condemns unrighteousness," Mozi wrote. "The will of Heaven is that men love and benefit one another." This theistic orientation made his philosophy uniquely similar to monotheistic ethical systems, unusual among classical Chinese philosophical traditions [10].

Mozi's pacifism manifested in his staunch opposition to aggressive warfare ("*Fei Gong*"). He dispatched envoys to dissuade rulers from military campaigns, while pragmatically supporting defensive engineering to protect vulnerable states from attack. His practical orientation extended to his critique of extravagant ceremonies and music ("*Fei Yue*")—beloved by Confucians—which he condemned as wasteful indulgences that diverted resources from the public good.

Rejecting the growing trend of fatalism ("*Fei Ming*") in Chinese thought, Mozi advocated for moral voluntarism—the belief that people shape their own virtue through effort and right action rather than submitting to predetermined fate. This stance reflected his broader commitment to pragmatic action over passive acceptance. "The way of universal love is the way of the sage-kings," Mozi declared, "The way that brings peace to the world, and the way that Heaven wants us to walk."

At its height during the Warring States period, Mohism rivaled Confucianism in influence. The school attracted followers primarily from the lower and middle strata of society—artisans, engineers, craftsmen, and those opposed to Confucian elitism. Smaller states threatened by powerful neighbors often welcomed Mohist advisors, who provided both ethical counsel and practical defensive strategies.

Despite its initial influence, the philosophy gradually lost ground after the Qin and Han unification of China in 221 BCE. The First Emperor's Legalist regime suppressed all rival philosophies [6], and the subsequent Han Dynasty eventually elevated Confucianism to state orthodoxy, with Daoism as the complementary inner path. Nevertheless, Mozi's advocacy for universal moral responsibility predated similar concepts in Western traditions like Stoicism and Christianity by centuries, giving his teachings a remarkably modern resonance [7].

Though Mohism faded as an independent school, its ideas persisted in various forms. The later Legalist tradition adopted aspects of Mohist utilitarianism, while Neo-Confucianism incorporated elements of Mohist rationalism. Some scholars have even suggested that aspects of Mohist universal love may have influenced the development of Chinese Buddhism, particularly its emphasis on compassion for all sentient beings.

Shang Yang and the Legalist School

During the tumultuous Warring States period, when China was fractured into competing powers, Shang Yang (also known as Gongsun Yang) emerged as one of history's most consequential political reformers. Unlike many philosophers of his era who merely theorized, Shang Yang implemented his vision as chief minister of the state of Qin, transforming it from a peripheral power into the kingdom that would eventually unify China[10]. Viewing both Confucians and Mohists as dangerous idealists clinging to outdated notions of virtue and benevolence, Shang Yang prioritized what he saw as practical necessities obedience, productivity, and military strength.

The Pillars of Legalist Philosophy

Legalism crystallized around three fundamental concepts that together formed a comprehensive theory of statecraft. The first principle, Fa (法) or Law, held that governance must be based on clear, public, and universally applied legal codes. "The laws must be made clear and the orders must be made trustworthy," states the Book of Lord Shang. Where Confucians believed moral cultivation would produce good rulers and subjects, Legalists insisted that people respond to incentives, not ideals.

The second principle, Shu (術) or Technique, encompassed the administrative methods rulers should employ to maintain control—surveillance systems, divided responsibilities among officials, and centralized decision-making. Even family members and close allies could not be trusted; the system, not personal relationships, must govern the state.

The third principle, Shi (勢) or Authority, reconceptualized the source of political power. Contrary to the Confucian emphasis on personal virtue (de, 德), Legalists argued that power resided in position and institutional authority. "It is the position that makes the man. Even a weak man becomes strong when placed in a position of control." This depersonalization of power meant that charisma and moral character were irrelevant compared to control over rewards and punishments. [6]

Reforms That Remade a State

Around 356 BCE and again in 350 BCE, Shang Yang implemented sweeping reforms in Qin that embodied Legalist principles. He established universal conscription, requiring all males to serve the state. He overhauled the taxation system to base it on productivity rather than social class. Perhaps most significantly, he instituted collective accountability, where families became responsible for each other's crimes, creating a society that policed itself through mutual surveillance [13].

These reforms were reinforced by harsh punishments designed to maintain public order through fear, and the active suppression of competing philosophies like Confucianism and Mohism [7]. The result was dramatic: Qin transformed into China's most formidable military power, eventually conquering all rival states under King Zheng, who became Qin Shi Huangdi, the First Emperor, in 221 BCE. In a striking illustration of Legalist impersonalism, Shang Yang himself was later executed under the very laws he had established when court politics turned against him [10].

A Contested Legacy

Legalism found adherents primarily among administrators and technocrats who valued efficiency over moral philosophy, and among rulers seeking order during chaotic times. However, it faced vehement opposition from Han Dynasty Confucians who viewed it as brutally pragmatic and spiritually empty, from Daoists who saw its control mechanisms as contrary to natural harmony, and from Mohists who condemned its amorality and cruelty.

Despite widespread rejection after the short-lived Qin Dynasty collapsed in 206 BCE, Legalist techniques of governance—bureaucratic hierarchies, standardized law codes, and centralized administration—became permanent features of Chinese imperial governance. Even as Confucianism regained ideological dominance during the Han Dynasty and beyond, the imperial state operated on mechanisms that were fundamentally Legalist in design, merely cloaked in Confucian ethical rhetoric. Thus, Chinese imperial administration for two millennia represented a pragmatic synthesis: Confucian in principle but Legalist in practice [10].

Chapter 1 - Endnotes

1. Sarah Allan, *The Shape of the Turtle: Myth, Art, and Cosmos in Early China* (Albany: State University of New York Press, 1991).

2. Lu Dagang, ed., *A New History of the Shijing* (Beijing: Zhonghua Book Company, 2006).

3. Kern, Martin. "Textual Transmission in Early China." In *Literature, Religion, and East Asia*, edited by Benjamin Elman et al., 23–45. Leiden: Brill, 2008.

4. Li Xueqin, "'*Baijia Zhengming' de Zhenshen Faduan* [The True Origin of 'Hundred Schools of Thought']", Shixue Yuekan 3 (1984).

5. Jennifer Robertson, *The Eclipse of the Confucian Moral Life* (Albany: SUNY Press, 2005).

6. A. C. Graham, *Disputers of the Tao: Philosophical Argument in Ancient China* (La Salle, IL: Open Court, 1989).

7. Chris Fraser, *Mozi: A Study and Translation* (Berlin: Walter de Gruyter, 1986).

8. D. C. Lau, *Mencius* (Harmondsworth: Penguin Books, 1970).

9. *Xunzi,* trans. Burton Watson (New York: Columbia University Press, 1968).

10. Wang, Aihe. *Cosmos and Governance: The Discourse of Heaven in Early China.* Cambridge: Cambridge University Press, 2014.

11. Bokenkamp, Stephen. *Early Daoist Scriptures.* Berkeley: University of California Press, 1997.

12. Robinet, Isabelle. *Taoism: Growth of a Religion.* Stanford: Stanford University Press, 1997.

13. Pines, Yuri. *The Everlasting Empire: The Political Culture of Ancient China*, Harvard University Press, 2012.

Chapter 2

Dao: The Way of the Mystics

As Confucian ideology became increasingly institutionalized in Chinese society, with its emphasis on social hierarchy, ritual propriety, and moral cultivation, a profoundly different philosophical current was quietly emerging from the forests, mountains, and remote valleys of ancient China. This tradition would come to be known as Daoism (or Taoism), a mystical philosophy that offered a radical alternative to the structured world of Confucian orthodoxy [1].

Where Confucian scholar-officials busied themselves with statecraft and ritual precision in the courts and academies, Daoist sages sought wisdom in wilderness retreats, often deliberately removing themselves from the centers of power and conventional society. This physical withdrawal mirrored their philosophical stance—a stepping back from the artificial constructs of civilization to reconnect with something more fundamental and primordial.

Mythical Foundations

The traditional account attributes the founding of philosophical Daoism to the semi-legendary figure Laozi (literally "Old Master"), supposedly an older contemporary of Confucius himself. According to tradition, Laozi served as an archivist in the Zhou court before becoming disillusioned with the corruption and artifice of political life [2]. He is said to have recorded his wisdom before disappearing from society, resulting in the cryptic and profound 5,000-character text known as the *Dao De Jing* (or *Tao Te Ching*).

The second foundational figure, Zhuangzi (Master Zhuang, c. 369-286 BCE), is more historically verifiable. Born as Zhuang Zhou in the state of Song during the Warring States period, he lived during an era when Confucian ideology was becoming increasingly dominant in intellectual circles. The text that bears his name, the *Zhuangzi*, presents a more elaborate, imaginative, and often humorous exposition of Daoist principles through parables, conversations, and surreal anecdotes [1].

Together, these two texts—the terse and enigmatic *Dao De Jing* and the expansive, playful *Zhuangzi*—form the philosophical core of early Daoism, a tradition that would evolve through the centuries into both a sophisticated philosophy and a complex religious system.

Laozi: The Old Master

The figure known as Laozi (老子), literally "Old Master" or "Ancient Child," stands as one of history's most enigmatic philosophical founders. Traditionally dated to the 6th century BCE as an elder contemporary of Confucius, Laozi exists at the intersection of history and legend, with his biography blending documented history, mythological elements, and philosophical symbolism.

According to traditional accounts recorded in Sima Qian's *Records of the Grand Historian* (c. 94 BCE), Laozi was born with the surname Li (李) and personal name Er (耳), in the state of Chu during the late Spring and Autumn period [3]. Legend holds that his mother carried him for 62 years before he emerged from her left side as an already elderly man with white hair—a supernatural origin story that symbolically establishes his profound wisdom from birth.

Modern scholarship suggests that rather than being a single historical figure, "Laozi" likely represents a composite persona that evolved over generations, possibly encompassing multiple thinkers whose insights were eventually attributed to a singular philosophical founder [1]. The text associated with him, the *Dao De Jing*, shows evidence of diverse authorship across different time periods, with linguistic analysis suggesting compilation sometime during the 4th-3rd centuries BCE—well after Laozi's traditional lifetime.

The Court Archivist

The classical account describes Laozi as having served as an archivist or "keeper of archives" at the Zhou royal court in Luoyang. This position would have given him unprecedented access to historical documents, ritual texts, and astronomical records—a comprehensive library of ancient Chinese wisdom [2]. This aspect of his biography symbolically positions Daoism not as a radical break from Chinese tradition but as emerging from its deepest roots, preceding even the formalized Confucian teachings.

The most famous story about Laozi recounts his meeting with Confucius, who supposedly sought out the older sage to inquire about ritual practices. After their encounter, Confucius is said to have remarked to his disciples: "Birds fly, fish swim, animals run. But the dragon is beyond my knowledge; it rises on the wind and clouds into heaven. Today I have seen Laozi, and he is like the dragon [1]."

This comparative mythology established the essential contrast between the two foundational philosophical traditions of China: Confucius as the exemplar of structured learning and social engagement versus Laozi as the embodiment of intuitive wisdom and transcendent detachment.

The Westward Journey

The most significant episode in Laozi's traditional biography occurs at its conclusion. Disillusioned with the moral decay of the Zhou kingdom and foreseeing its collapse, the aging sage decided to withdraw from civilization entirely. Traveling westward on a water buffalo toward what is now Tibet or India, he approached the Hangu Pass at China's western frontier.

There, the gatekeeper Yin Xi (sometimes called Guan Yin) recognized the extraordinary nature of this humble traveler. Knowing that a sage was about to depart from the world, the guard implored Laozi to leave behind some record of his wisdom before disappearing into the wilderness beyond China's borders.

In response to this request, Laozi is said to have composed on the spot a concise text of approximately 5,000 Chinese characters, divided into 81 brief chapters. This work would become known as the *Dao De Jing* (道德經), sometimes translated as "The Classic of the Way and Its Power" or "The Book of the Way and Its Virtue"—one of the most influential mystical texts in human history [1,2].

After completing this text, the Old Master continued westward and vanished from historical record, with some traditions claiming he traveled to India where he may have influenced (or even become) the Buddha. Others suggest he achieved physical immortality and still dwells in the mountains as a perfected being. This mysterious departure reinforces the central Daoist principle of returning to the formless origin of all being.

The Immortal Text

Whatever the historical reality behind Laozi's biography, the text attributed to him begins with a paradox that establishes its fundamental orientation toward ineffable reality:

"The Dao that can be spoken is not the eternal Dao. The name that can be named is not the eternal name."

These opening lines immediately signal that what follows is not conventional philosophy but a pointer toward mystical experience beyond the reach of language and conceptual thought [1]. Through spare, poetic language filled with natural imagery and paradoxical formulations, the *Dao De Jing* outlines a vision of ultimate reality and human flourishing radically different from the social and ethical focus of Confucianism.

The text resolves into two primary thematic dimensions, reflected in its title:

Dao (道): The *Way*—primordial, spontaneous, ineffable; the Dao is portrayed not as a deity or supreme being, but as the source of all being—an unnameable principle that precedes and pervades the manifest universe. Unlike the anthropomorphic Heaven of early Chinese religion or the moral Heaven (Tian) of Confucian thought [1], the Dao operates without intention or effort:

"The Dao never does anything, yet through it all things are done." — *Dao De Jing*, ch. 37

This cosmological principle gives rise to heaven and earth yet does not interfere with their natural operations. It acts without acting, achieves without striving, and maintains order through an innate harmony rather than through command or control. The sage who aligns with the Dao emulates this quality of non-interference while remaining deeply effective.

"The Dao is empty (like a bowl). It may be used but its capacity is never exhausted. It is bottomless, perhaps the ancestor of all things.... Deep and still, it appears to exist forever." — *Dao De Jing*, ch. 4

<u>De (德)</u>: Virtue or inner power—not moral virtue, but integrity; the second key concept, *De*, represents not conventional virtue or morality but a kind of innate power or integrity that arises from alignment with the Dao. Unlike Confucian virtue, which is cultivated through education and ritual practice, Daoist *De* emerges naturally when artificial restraints and distinctions are removed.

"Superior virtue is not virtuous, and thus has virtue. Inferior virtue never strays from virtue, and thus has no virtue. Superior virtue does nothing, yet nothing is left undone. Inferior virtue acts, and has intent to act." — *Dao De Jing*, ch. 38

This inner power manifests as a kind of magnetic charisma or natural authority that influences without imposing, accomplishes without striving, and leads without commanding [2]. It represents the embodiment of Dao principles in human life—a deep harmony with the natural order that enables effortless effectiveness in all domains of experience.

Legacy and Influence

By the Han dynasty (206 BCE–220 CE), Laozi had been elevated to divine status as "Lord Lao" (Laojun), one of the Three Pure Ones in religious Daoism [2]. Temples were established in his honor, and elaborate hagiographies expanded his biography to include miraculous births and transcendent powers.

The *Dao De Jing* significantly influenced Chinese Buddhism, especially the Chan and later Zen schools, which integrated Daoist ideas of naturalness (*ziran*) and non-action (*wu wei*) into their path to enlightenment [1]. Among world classics, the Dao De Jing is one of the most translated and widely read texts, second perhaps only to the Bible in global influence. In modern times, it continues to reach millions of readers worldwide.

Whether understood as a historical figure, a composite persona, or a purely legendary sage, Laozi embodies the Daoist ideal—someone whose influence operates not through assertion and control but through subtlety and the paradoxical power of yielding. As the *Dao De Jing* itself observes:

"The sage stays behind, thus he is ahead. He is detached, thus at one with all. Through selfless action, he attains fulfillment." — *Dao De Jing*, ch. 7

Zhuangzi (Chuang Tzu): The Sage Who Dreamed He Was a Butterfly

Unlike the semi-legendary Laozi, Zhuangzi (莊子, ca. 369–286 BCE) stands on firmer historical ground. Born as Zhuang Zhou in the state of Song during the tumultuous Warring States period, he lived during an era of intense philosophical ferment and political upheaval. While biographical details remain sparse, historical records indicate he served briefly as a minor official in the lacquer garden of Meng, though he primarily lived as a private scholar of modest means.

Contemporary with Mencius, the great expositor of Confucianism, Zhuangzi developed a radically different philosophical vision—one that questioned the very foundations of conventional knowledge, morality, and social order. His historical context is crucial to understanding his work; as the various states of China engaged in ever more destructive warfare and political machinations, Zhuangzi responded not with practical reforms or moral exhortations, but with a profound questioning of the categories and distinctions that underlie political and ethical discourse itself [1].

According to tradition, King Wei of Chu once sent messengers to offer Zhuangzi a position as prime minister. The philosopher responded by asking the messengers about a sacred tortoise kept in the king's temple, which was honored and preserved after its death. "This tortoise," Zhuangzi asked, "would it rather be dead and have its remains venerated, or alive and dragging its tail in the mud?" When the messengers admitted it would prefer to be alive, Zhuangzi replied, "Begone! I, too, prefer to drag my tail in the mud." This anecdote captures his preference for natural freedom over social position, a central theme throughout his writings.

The Text and Its Structure

The book that bears his name, the *Zhuangzi* (also known as the *Nanhua Zhenjing* or "True Classic of Southern Florescence"), comprises 33 chapters traditionally divided into three sections.

<u>Inner Chapters</u> (1-7): Generally considered to be written by Zhuangzi himself, these chapters contain the most important philosophical insights and the most brilliant literary expressions of his thought.

<u>Outer Chapters</u> (8-22): Likely written by direct disciples, these chapters elaborate on themes from the Inner Chapters while sometimes showing influences from other philosophical traditions.

<u>Miscellaneous Chapters</u> (23-33): Probably compiled later from various sources, these chapters show greater diversity of viewpoint, including some that appear to blend Daoist and Confucian perspectives.

While the text as a whole represents a school of thought rather than the work of a single author, the distinctive voice and philosophical vision of the Inner Chapters reveal a mind of extraordinary creativity and insight—a thinker who expanded Laozi's cryptic aphorisms into philosophical fables, paradoxes, and allegories of unparalleled imagination and depth.

Zhuangzi: Literary Genius

Where the *Dao De Jing* is spare and enigmatic, the *Zhuangzi* overflows with wit, dreamlike imagery, and startling juxtapositions. Its pages are populated by talking animals, argumentative philosophers, supernatural beings, and eccentric sages who challenge conventional wisdom through outrageous behavior. Zhuangzi employed this rich literary arsenal not merely as ornamentation but as the perfect vehicle for a philosophy that questions the boundaries between categories and celebrates the transformative power of imagination.

His prose style shifts effortlessly between philosophical dialogue, mythic narrative, poetry, and what might be called philosophical comedy—moments of absurdist humor that serve to jolt readers out of their habitual patterns of thought [1]. Consider his story of Confucius instructing an ambitious disciple to study with a "madman" who sings at his wife's grave, or his tale of the hideous yet mysteriously charismatic Ugly Tuo who attracts more followers than the most handsome men in the state.

This literary virtuosity serves a profound philosophical purpose. By destabilizing our expectations, blurring boundaries between reality and fantasy, and employing paradox and contradiction, Zhuangzi's text enacts the very philosophical perspective it advocates—a perspective in which fixed categories dissolve into fluid transformation and conventional distinctions give way to a more spacious awareness. Let us examine Zhuangzi's Key Ideas.

Transformation of Things – All is in Flux

Central to Zhuangzi's worldview is the recognition that reality is characterized not by fixed essences but by continuous transformation (*hua*, 化) [1]. In the chapter "On the Equality of Things," he writes:

"There is nothing that is not the 'other,' nothing that is not 'it.' If you look at something from the standpoint of 'the other,' you do not see it; only when you know it from your own standpoint do you know it. Thus it is said: 'The other' arises out of 'it,' and 'it' arises out of 'the other.'"

For Zhuangzi, categories like "life" and "death," "self" and "other," "beautiful" and "ugly" are not absolute but provisional, useful for certain limited purposes but ultimately dissolving into a more fundamental unity. This perspective is not simply theoretical but has profound existential implications, particularly in facing mortality [2].

"How do I know that loving life is not a delusion? How do I know that in hating death I am not like a man who, having left home in his youth, has forgotten the way back? Lady Li was the daughter of the border guard of Ai. When the state of Jin first got her, she wept until her tears drenched her collar. But after she came to the palace, shared the king's bed, and ate rich food, she regretted her tears. How do I know that the dead do not regret their previous longing for life?"

This radical questioning of our most basic assumptions about identity and value opens a space for a more fluid and responsive engagement with existence—one not bound by rigid categories or fixed narratives about what constitutes the good life.

The Dream of the Butterfly – Identity is Fluid

Perhaps the most famous passage in the *Zhuangzi* is the butterfly dream, which appears in the second chapter:

"Once, Zhuang Zhou dreamed he was a butterfly, fluttering about, happy with himself and doing as he pleased. He didn't know he was Zhuang Zhou. Suddenly he woke up and there he was, solid and unmistakable Zhuang Zhou. But he didn't know if he was

Zhuang Zhou who had dreamt he was a butterfly, or a butterfly dreaming he was Zhuang Zhou. Between Zhuang Zhou and the butterfly, there must be some distinction! This is called the Transformation of Things."

This deceptively simple anecdote raises profound questions about consciousness, identity, and the nature of reality itself [1]. Did Zhuangzi dream he was a butterfly, or is the butterfly now dreaming it is Zhuangzi? The point is not to resolve this paradox but to dwell within the space of uncertainty it creates—a space where identity is revealed as fundamentally fluid and provisional.

The butterfly dream suggests that the boundaries of selfhood are permeable, that consciousness might flow between forms, and that our ordinary waking certainty about who we are may be no more stable than the apparent certainty we feel within a dream. This perspective does not lead to nihilism or despair but rather to a kind of freedom—a playful engagement with identity that allows for creative transformation rather than anxious self-preservation [4].

The Useless Tree – Value Beyond Utility

In a culture increasingly dominated by utilitarian concerns—whether Confucian social utility or Mohist economic utility—Zhuangzi offered a radical critique through parables like that of the useless tree [1].

"Hui Tzu said to Zhuangzi, 'I have a big tree of the kind men call *shu*. Its trunk is too gnarled and bumpy to apply a measuring line to, its branches too bent and twisty to match with a compass or square. You could stand it by the road and no carpenter would look at it twice. Your words, too, are big and useless, and so everyone alike spurns them!'

Zhuangzi replied, 'Have you ever seen a wildcat or a weasel? It crouches down and hides, waiting for something to come along. It leaps here and there, east and west, not hesitating to go high or low—until it falls into the trap and dies in the net. Then again there's the yak, big as a cloud hanging from the sky. It certainly knows how to be big, though it doesn't know how to catch rats. Now you have this big tree and you're distressed because it's useless. Why not plant it in Not-Even-Anything Village, or the field of Broad-and-Boundless, relax and do nothing by its side, or lie down for a free and easy sleep under it? Axes will never shorten its life, nothing can ever harm it. If there's no use for it, how can it come to grief or pain?'"

A tree is "useless" to carpenters but thrives untouched precisely because of this apparent defect. What appears "useless" by narrow human standards may be closest to the Dao—free from instrumental exploitation and able to fulfill its natural lifespan. This parable challenges the pervasive assumption that value comes from utility, suggesting instead that there is profound worth in that which serves no external purpose [2].

This theme appears repeatedly throughout the *Zhuangzi*, from the story of the huge gnarled tree venerated as a shrine, to the tale of Crippled Shu whose physical deformity exempts him from conscription during wartime. These narratives invite us to consider whether our conventional standards of value might actually be inverted—whether what we reject as "useless" might, from another perspective, be most aligned with the Dao's spontaneous authenticity.

Against Morality and Hierarchy – Beyond Distinctions

While Confucians elaborated complex moral codes and social hierarchies, and Mohists proposed universal standards of benefit, Zhuangzi questioned the very foundation of moral and social distinctions [1]. He saw conventional morality not as the solution to human conflict but as its source.

"In the world, everyone knows to seek knowledge that they do not have, but no one knows to seek what they already know. Everyone knows to condemn what they dislike, but no one knows to condemn what they have already formed preferences about. This is what leads to great disorder."

For Zhuangzi, conventional distinctions—between good and bad, noble and base, beautiful and ugly—arise from limited perspective rather than absolute truth. He illustrated this through countless parables about the relativity of perspective: what is medicine to one creature is poison to another; what appears as a vast ocean to a frog in a well is but a puddle to those with broader vision.

The truly wise, according to Zhuangzi, are those who can "roam in the realm beyond distinctions"—who can navigate the world with fluid responsiveness rather than rigid adherence to fixed categories [4].

"The perfect man has no self; The spiritual man has no merit; The sage has no fame." — *Zhuangzi*, Ch. 1

This stance does not imply moral nihilism but rather points toward a more fundamental ethical orientation—one based on spontaneous attunement to circumstances rather than rule-following or virtue signaling. The true sage responds appropriately to each unique situation without being constrained by pre-established moral formulas or social expectations.

Skillful Living — The Hidden Center of Zhuangzi's Philosophy

Beyond his critique of conventional knowledge and morality lies what might be considered Zhuangzi's positive vision—a conception of skillful living illustrated through stories of exemplary practitioners: Cook Ding who butchers oxen with such attunement that his blade never dulls; the wheelwright who can feel the right way to carve a wheel but cannot express it in words; the swimmer who moves through dangerous rapids as if they were his natural element.

These "knack stories" reveal a common pattern: mastery comes not through analytical thinking or rule-following but through a direct, embodied engagement with reality that transcends conceptual understanding [1]. The skilled practitioner enters a state where the boundaries between self and activity dissolve, where action arises spontaneously in perfect attunement with circumstance.

This ideal of skillful living represents not a withdrawal from life but a more profound engagement with it—one freed from the constraints of self-consciousness, social convention, and instrumental rationality. It points toward what Zhuangzi calls "the free and easy wandering" or "carefree roaming" (*xiaoyao you*)—a way of moving through the world with spontaneous grace rather than anxious striving [4].

Legacy and Influence

Zhuangzi's influence extends far beyond philosophical Daoism. His celebration of spontaneity, skepticism toward language and conventional knowledge, and literary brilliance profoundly shaped Chinese arts, particularly poetry, painting, and what would later become Chan Buddhism [5]. The "eccentric" tradition in Chinese culture—from hermit poets to mad Zen masters—owes much to his valorization of the unusual, the marginal, and the authentically idiosyncratic [2].

Perhaps most significantly, Zhuangzi offered a profound alternative to the dominant intellectual traditions of his time—an alternative that prized freedom over order, spontaneity over discipline, humor over solemnity, and open-ended questioning over doctrinal certainty. In a world increasingly shaped by instrumental rationality and utilitarian value, his vision of "carefree wandering" continues to offer a necessary counterbalance—a reminder that the deepest dimensions of human experience transcend the categories through which we habitually organize our understanding of reality [4].

As he himself wrote in what might serve as both epitaph and invitation:

"The fish trap exists because of the fish; once you've gotten the fish, you can forget the trap. The rabbit snare exists because of the rabbit; once you've gotten the rabbit, you can forget the snare. Words exist because of meaning; once you've gotten the meaning, you can forget the words. Where can I find a person who has forgotten words so I can have a word with them?"

Philosophical Tenets of Daoism

Rejection of Conventional Society

In a direct challenge to the Confucian project of social engineering through ritual and moral education, the Daoist sages abandoned the world of names, hierarchies, and ceremonies. They saw such constructs not as solutions to disorder but as its very source [1].

"The more prohibitions there are, the poorer the people will be. The more sharp weapons there are, the more confusions there will be in the state. The more skills of technique, the more cunning things will be brought forth. The more laws there are, the more thieves and robbers there will be." — *Dao De Jing*, ch. 57

This critique extended to language itself, which the Daoists viewed as an inadequate tool for capturing ultimate reality—an imposition of artificial categories upon the seamless unity of existence [2].

Where Confucius sought to "rectify the names" (*zhengming*) to ensure that language properly reflected reality, the Daoists suggested that this project was fundamentally misguided. True wisdom began with recognizing the limitations of conceptual thinking and linguistic categories altogether.

Nature as Teacher

While Confucians looked to ancient sages and historical texts for moral guidance, the Daoists turned to a different source of wisdom: the patterns and processes of the natural world. This was not nature as an object of scientific study, but nature as a living manifestation of the Dao itself—the spontaneous, self-organizing intelligence that permeates all existence [6].

"Man follows the earth. Earth follows heaven. Heaven follows the Dao. The Dao follows what is natural." — *Dao De Jing*, ch. 25

By observing how water flows to the lowest places yet ultimately overcomes the hardest stone, how the seasons cycle without effort or intention, how animals live without moral precepts yet maintain natural harmony, the Daoist sage discovered a profound alternative to the strained virtue of Confucian self-cultivation [1].

"The highest good is like water. Water benefits the ten thousand things without striving. It settles in places that people disdain. Thus, it is like the Dao." — *Dao De Jing*, ch. 8

This natural wisdom manifests as *ziran* (自然), often translated as "spontaneity" or "naturalness," but perhaps best understood as the uncontrived authenticity that emerges when beings act in accordance with their inherent nature rather than according to artificial standards or external pressures.

The Inversion of Values

Where Confucius cultivated speech, action, and social duty, the mystics prized silence, emptiness, and non-action (*wu wei*, 无为). This represented not merely a different set of virtues but a fundamental inversion of conventional values [4].

"The five colors blind the eye. The five tones deafen the ear. The five flavors dull the taste. Racing and hunting madden the mind. Precious things lead one astray. Therefore the sage is guided by what he feels and not by what he sees. He lets go of that and chooses this." — *Dao De Jing*, ch. 12

In a society increasingly defined by scholarly achievement, ritual precision, and moral striving, the Daoists proposed a radical alternative: unlearning conventional wisdom, emptying oneself of ambition and knowledge, and returning to a state of original simplicity.

"In the pursuit of learning, every day something is acquired. In the pursuit of the Dao, every day something is dropped." — *Dao De Jing*, ch. 48

Mystic Tenets

The philosophical core of Daoism can be distilled into several interconnected concepts, each representing an aspect of its mystical philosophy. As we saw in the section about the *Dao De Jing* by Laozi, two of these tenets are *Dao*, and *De*, reflected in the title of the book. To these we will add a number of others, like Wu-wei and Ziran which represent effortlessness and naturalness.

Dao (道) – The Way; ultimate reality.

The Dao is the central mystery at the heart of Daoist philosophy—simultaneously the origin of all things, the process by which they unfold, and the destination to which they return. Unlike the anthropomorphic Heaven (*Tian*) of Confucian thought, the Dao transcends personification. The Dao is both transcendent and immanent—beyond all conceptual categories yet intimately present in the most ordinary aspects of existence. It operates according to principles fundamentally different from human intention or design [6].

De (德) -- Virtue or inner power

De in Daoism refers to an innate inner power or integrity that arises from living in harmony with the Dao. Unlike Confucian virtue, which is cultivated through deliberate action and social rituals, De emerges spontaneously when artificial distinctions and intentions are released. It is effortless virtue—a magnetic presence or quiet authority that influences without force, acts without striving, and embodies the Dao through natural alignment. As the Dao De Jing (ch. 38) puts it, true virtue does not try to be virtuous—hence, it truly is [1,2].

Wu wei (无为) – Non-doing; effortless action.

Perhaps the most distinctive and misunderstood of Daoist concepts is *wu wei*, often translated as "non-action" but better understood as action that arises naturally without forced effort or self-conscious striving. It is not passivity or inertia but a form of effortless effectiveness that emerges when one acts in harmony with the inherent tendencies of things In the political realm, this manifested as a minimalist approach to governance that contrasted sharply with the activist Confucian model [5,6].

"The sage does without doing, teaches without talking. The ten thousand things rise and fall without cease, Creating, yet not possessing, Working, yet not taking credit. Work is done, then forgotten. Therefore it lasts forever." — *Dao De Jing*, ch. 2

Zhuangzi illustrated *wu wei* through stories of artisans so attuned to their craft that they worked beyond technique, entering a flow state where the distinction between doer and deed dissolved. His famous butcher Ding cut oxen with such natural precision that his blade never dulled, moving through the spaces between the joints rather than forcing his way through bones and tissues.

Ziran (自然) – Naturalness; authentic unfolding

Ziran, literally "self-so," refers to the quality of natural authenticity that arises when beings act according to their inherent nature rather than according to artificial standards. The term implies both spontaneity and a kind of inner-directed autonomy that stands in contrast to the externally oriented discipline of Confucian self-cultivation.

This concept extends from individual conduct to social and political organization. Where Confucians believed that order must be imposed through ritual, education, and moral example, Daoists suggested that the most profound order emerges organically when artificial constraints are removed [6].

"When the great Dao is forgotten, Goodness and piety appear. When intelligence and knowledge arise, Great hypocrisy follows." — *Dao De Jing*, ch. 18

Wú (無 / 无) – Non-being; Nothingness

Often translated as "non-being", wú also implies emptiness, absence, or the unspeakable origin of all things. In Daoist cosmology, wú is the source of Dao—it is the silent, pre-conceptual ground of reality [1]. In this context, wú is a kind of pregnant silence, the ineffable from which all names and forms arise.

"All things in the world come from being (有); Being comes from non-being (無)."— Dao De Jing, Chapter 40

Wú is the empty origin from which all things arise and to which they return. Being and non-being are not seen as opposites, but as interdependent aspects of reality.

Wú is also a state of inner emptiness, often cultivated through Zhuangzi's "fasting of the heart" (心齋 xīn zhāi) or quiet sitting (靜坐 jingzuò). Wú symbolizes the still point, the mystical source, and the true reality behind appearances [6].

Jing (靜) – "Stillness" / "Quietude"

Jing implies both inner silence and cosmic stillness, often paired with xu (虛) meaning "emptiness." Xu-Jing (虛靜) is a compound that means "empty and still"—the ideal mental state for aligning with the Dao [2]. This state is a return to inner equilibrium, beyond emotional disturbance or intellectual distraction.

In a tradition that prized scholarly eloquence and moral instruction, the Daoists valued a paradoxical kind of knowing beyond words—an intuitive apprehension of reality unmediated by conceptual thought.

"Those who know do not speak. Those who speak do not know." — *Dao De Jing*, ch. 56

This skepticism toward language reflected a deeper epistemological stance that questioned the ability of discursive reasoning to capture the fluid, ever-changing nature of reality [4]. In the *Zhuangzi*, this culminates in stories where the deepest insights are conveyed not through philosophical argument but through silences, dreams, and even the spaces between words.

There is a classical Daoist phrase: "the teaching of no words", which is often attributed to Laozi and was adopted by Zhuangzi and later by Chan Buddhism. It expresses the highest form of transmission: not through doctrines or logic, but by non-verbal resonance, gesture, paradox, or silent presence.

"The greatest teaching is wordless; the Way cannot be told." — *Zhuangzi*, Ch. 3

Legacy and Evolution

The tension between Confucian and Daoist tendencies would become a defining feature of Chinese civilization, with each tradition serving as a necessary complement and corrective to the other. While Confucianism dominated official life—government, education, and social ethics—Daoism offered a refuge from the pressures of hierarchy and convention, a space for artistic creativity, spiritual exploration, and philosophical critique [1].

Over the centuries, Daoism would evolve far beyond its philosophical origins. By the Eastern Han dynasty (25-220 CE), organized Daoist religious movements emerged, complete with temples, priesthoods, deities, rituals, and elaborate practices aimed at physical immortality and spiritual transcendence [2]. Despite these developments, the core philosophical insights of Laozi and Zhuangzi continued to influence Chinese art, poetry, landscape painting, medicine, and martial arts [1].

The subtle interplay between Confucian structure and Daoist spontaneity, between social engagement and mystical withdrawal, created a dynamic balance that allowed Chinese civilization to endure through millennia of political and social change. As the *Dao De Jing* suggests:

"The rigid and inflexible will surely fall; The soft and yielding will overcome." — *Dao De Jing*, ch. 76

In a world increasingly dominated by Confucian hierarchies and rituals, the mystic schools offered not just an alternative philosophical stance but a necessary reminder of what lies beyond the world of names and forms—the ineffable Dao that gives rise to the ten thousand things yet remains eternally mysterious and complete within itself.

Chapter 2: Endnotes

1. A. C. Graham, *Disputers of the Tao: Philosophical Argument in Ancient China* (La Salle, IL: Open Court, 1989).
2. Robinet, Isabelle. *Taoism: Growth of a Religion.* Stanford: Stanford University Press, 1997.
3. Sima Qian. *Records of the Grand Historian*, trans. Burton Watson. New York: Columbia University Press, 1993.
4. Ziporyn, Brook. *Zhuangzi: The Essential Writings with Selections from Traditional Commentaries.* Hackett, 2009. [New]
5. Dumoulin, Heinrich. *Zen Buddhism: A History*, Vol. 1: India and China. Bloomington: World Wisdom, 2005.
6. Kohn, Livia. *The Daoist Tradition: An Introduction.* 2nd ed. Boulder: Shambhala Publications, 2020.

CHAPTER 3

Yin-Yang: The Cosmic Polarity

The concept of *Yin-Yang* (陰陽) represents one of the most enduring and profound contributions of Chinese thought to world philosophy. While popularly recognized as a symbol, its depth as a philosophical framework for understanding reality extends far beyond its iconic black-and-white representation.

Pre-Systematic Origins

Long before its formal theorization, the seeds of Yin-Yang thinking emerged in China's earliest recorded thoughts:

The I Ching (易經, *Yijing*, Book of Changes), dating from at least the Western Zhou period (1046-771 BCE), contains the fundamental binary thinking that would evolve into Yin-Yang philosophy. Its system of broken and unbroken lines (representing yin and yang qualities) arranged in trigrams and hexagrams provided a framework for understanding cosmic patterns [1].

Oracle bone inscriptions from the Shang Dynasty (c. 1600-1046 BCE) reveal earlier associations of natural polarities: day/night, summer/winter, heat/cold. These were not yet systematized into a coherent philosophy but show the nascent recognition of complementary forces in nature [2].

Agricultural observations played a crucial role in developing this worldview. Early Chinese farmers meticulously tracked the interplay between light and shadow, warmth and cold, growth and dormancy—practical experiences that informed cosmic understanding [3].

The *Shang shu* (尚書, Book of Documents) and *Shi jing* (詩經, Book of Poetry) contain early references to heaven and earth as complementary cosmic powers, foreshadowing the more sophisticated Yin-Yang cosmology that would emerge later [5].

The original meanings of the terms are revealing: "yin" referred to the shaded side of a mountain, while "yang" denoted the sunny side. This simple geographical observation gradually expanded to encompass all complementary cosmic phenomena.

During the tumultuous Warring States period (475-221 BCE), as competing philosophical schools vied for influence, the Yin-Yang School (*Yinyang jia*, 陰陽家) emerged as a distinct tradition of cosmological thought. This school was primarily concerned with understanding the patterns of the natural world and their implications for human affairs.

Zou Yan (鄒衍, c. 305-240 BCE), often credited as the school's founder, synthesized existing ideas about cosmology, astronomy, and the cyclical patterns of nature into a comprehensive system. Historical records in the *Shiji* (史記, Records of the Grand Historian) describe him as "investigating the confluences and dispersals of the Six Qi, the successes and failures of the past and present, even the transformations of the strange and the normal."

Zou Yan developed what later historians would call the "Theory of the Three Powers" (*sancai*, 三才)—Heaven, Earth, and Humanity—integrated through the dynamic principles of Yin and Yang [2]. His teaching secured imperial patronage and spread throughout the various states of pre-imperial China.

The Guanzi (管子) text, though attributed to the much earlier statesman Guan Zhong (管仲, d. 645 BCE), contains significant Yin-Yang philosophical material likely added during the 4th-3rd centuries BCE. Its chapter "Inner Work" (*Neiye*, 內業) represents one of the earliest systematic treatments of Yin-Yang applied to self-cultivation and governance [6].

Integration with the Five Phases Theory

A crucial development in the maturation of Yin-Yang philosophy was its integration with the Five Phases theory (*wuxing*, 五行).

These five phases—Wood, Fire, Earth, Metal, and Water—were understood not as static elements but as dynamic stages in ongoing cycles of transformation. The relationship between Yin-Yang and the Five Phases was conceptualized as hierarchical; Yin and Yang represent the primary cosmic division, while the Five Phases represent a more detailed subdivision of cosmic processes [1,3].

Each phase contains its own Yin and Yang aspects. For example, Fire is predominantly Yang but contains Yin within it. The phases interact in cycles of generation (*sheng*, 生) and of conquest (*ke*, 克), creating complex patterns of cosmic change governed by the alternation of Yin and Yang. This integrated cosmology provided ancient Chinese thinkers with a sophisticated framework for understanding everything from seasonal changes to political dynasties, from bodily processes to alchemical transformations.

Defining Yin and Yang

At their core, Yin and Yang represent complementary cosmic forces whose interaction produces and sustains all phenomena. They are not substances but qualities, patterns of movement, or energetic tendencies. Neither exists in absolute form; rather, they are relative terms describing relationships and processes [3].

Yin (陰) encompasses:	Yang (陽) encompasses:
Feminine qualities	Masculine qualities
Receptivity, passivity, and containment	Activity, creativity, and expression
Earth, darkness, night, autumn, and winter	Heaven, brightness, day, spring, and summer
Coolness, moisture, and descent	Warmth, dryness, and ascent
Inward movement, contraction, and conservation	Outward movement, expansion, and growth
Structure, form, and materiality	Function, energy, and transformation
The moon, water, valleys, and the north-facing slope	The sun, fire, mountains, and the south-facing slope
Intuition, emotion, and the unconscious	Intellect, logic, and consciousness
Rest, storage, and potential	Movement, expenditure, and manifestation

The *Huainanzi* (淮南子), an important Han Dynasty compendium of thought compiled around 139 BCE, describes their relationship: "Yin in its highest form is freezing while Yang in its highest form is boiling. The chilliness comes from Heaven and the warmth comes from Earth. The interaction of these two creates harmony, and thus things are born" [6].

Principles of Yin-Yang Relationship

The relationship between Yin and Yang is governed by several key principles that distinguish it from Western dualistic thinking. Yin and Yang define each other and cannot exist independently. As the Daodejing (道德經) states: "Being and non-being generate each other."

They exist in constant tension and perpetual rebalancing, never in static equilibrium. At their extremes, Yin transforms into Yang and Yang into Yin. The *Zhuangzi* (莊子) observes: "That which is killed is also born; that which is born is also killed [1]."

Yin and Yang are infinitely subdivided, so that within any Yin phenomenon is Yang, and within that Yang is Yin, ad infinitum—creating fractal-like complexity. Further, what is Yin in one context may be Yang in another. No phenomenon is absolutely Yin or absolutely Yang.

They follow a natural rhythm of alternation, like day following night, seasons changing, or breath moving in and out. The *Yijing* commentary states: "One Yin, one Yang—this is the Dao [7]." This pithy statement captures the essential understanding that reality itself is constituted by the dynamic interplay of these polar forces.

Naturalist Cosmology

The Yin-Yang School developed a sophisticated naturalist cosmology that went far beyond simple binaries. The scholars of this tradition—sometimes called *fangshi* (方士, "masters of methods")—created an intricate model of cosmic processes that included correspondences between microcosm and macrocosm (human body and cosmos) and numerological patterns that revealed cosmic rhythms (especially centered around numbers 5 and 8) [3].

These scholars also created seasonal calculations for agriculture, ritual, and governance, prediction systems based on cosmic cycles, and medical theories based on balance and harmony between Yin and Yang forces [4].

The Han Dynasty text *Huangdi Neijing* (黃帝內經, The Yellow Emperor's Inner Classic) exemplifies this developed cosmology, particularly in its opening dialogue between the Yellow Emperor and his minister Qi Bo:

"The Yellow Emperor asked: 'I have heard that in ancient times the people lived to be over a hundred years, and yet they remained active and did not become decrepit in their activities. But nowadays people reach only half of that age and yet become decrepit and failing. Is it because the world changes from generation to generation? Or is it that people have lost their proper way? [4]'

Qi Bo answered: 'In ancient times those people who understood the Dao patterned themselves upon the Yin and the Yang, and they lived in harmony with the arts of divination...[4]'"

Cosmological Framework

The Yin-Yang cosmology positioned humanity within a tripartite universe, consisting of heaven, earth, and humanity:

Heaven (天, *tian*)	Earth (地, *di*):	Humanity (人, *ren*)
The realm of cosmic patterns, celestial bodies, and Yang energy.	The realm of material manifestation, geography, and Yin energy.	The intermediary realm that participates in both Heaven and Earth.

The relationship between these three powers (*sancai*, 三才) was not hierarchical but harmonious—each needed the others. This framework established a cosmic ecology that emphasized interconnection rather than transcendence or dominion [1].

The *Lüshi Chunqiu* (呂氏春秋, Master Lü's Spring and Autumn Annals), compiled around 239 BCE, explains: "Heaven has its seasons, Earth has its resources, and humans have their governance. This is how they are able to form the Three Powers [8]."

A crucial concept in Yin-Yang cosmology is *ganying* (感應)—"stimulus and response" or "cosmic resonance." This principle holds that similar categories of phenomena naturally affect one another through sympathetic vibration, like two strings tuned to the same pitch. The concept explains how celestial events could influence earthly affairs, how music could affect human emotions and natural phenomena, and even how political virtue virtue (or its lack) could influence weather patterns. Because of the relationship between the forces, properly timed actions could harmonize with cosmic cycles [3].

The Book of Rites (禮記, *Liji*) states: "The vital energy of Heaven and Earth can be conducted to fullness or exhaustion. The vital energy of the human body can be made to respond by becoming full or empty. The sage, by understanding these principles, is able to establish the foundations of ritual and to harmonize actions [4]."

The *Guanzi* (管子) represents a crucial text in the development of Chinese philosophical synthesis. While attributed to Guan Zhong (管仲), the 7th century BCE prime minister of the state of Qi, textual analysis reveals it to be a compilation from the 4th-3rd centuries BCE, with some sections possibly dating as late as the Han Dynasty.

Its significance lies in its harmonization of philosophical currents:
- Daoist metaphysics of the Dao and non-action
- Legalist governance with practical statecraft
- Yin-Yang cosmology applied to both body and state
- Agrarian economic theories focused on resource management

The text consists of 86 chapters covering topics from military strategy to meditation practices, from economic policies to cosmological speculation. Its eclectic nature makes it a valuable window into the pre-imperial intellectual synthesis occurring in China [5].

Philosophical Integration

The Guanzi's integration of Yin-Yang theory with governance and self-cultivation appears most prominently in chapters like "Inner Work" (*Neiye*, 內業) and "Techniques of the Mind" (*Xinshu*, 心術):

"When your body is not aligned, The inner power will not come. When you are not tranquil within, Your mind will not be ordered. Align your body, assist the inner power, Then it will gradually come on its own" [9].

Here we see Yin-Yang harmony applied to mental cultivation, with the balancing of inner stillness (Yin) and vital energy (Yang) as the path to wisdom. In political philosophy, the Guanzi adapts Yin-Yang thinking to advocate for a ruler who embodies both Yang and Yin qualities: Yang qualities qualities for decisive action, clear laws, strong defense, and Yin qualities for receptivity to advice, conservation of resources, and subtle observation.

One passage advises: "*The enlightened ruler is empty and still, yet his subordinates work diligently. He is serene and unfathomable, yet his people do not grow confused*" [9].

The Integration of Yin-Yang into Daoism

While Yin-Yang theory and Daoism began as distinct traditions, their eventual integration created one of the most sophisticated philosophical systems in Chinese history. The convergence occurred gradually. Before the Han Dynasty they were relative independent, with occasional borrowing of concepts. The Western Han Dynasty (206 BCE-9 CE) was increasing cross-fertilization, and in the Eastern Han Dynasty (25-220 CE) they became substantially integrated.

By the Six Dynasties Period (220-589 CE), there was a complete synthesis between Ying-Yang and Dao, resulting in religious Daoism. Before that, they already shared many features. Both traditions emphasized natural patterns over human conventions, criticized Confucian ritualism and social hierarchies. Both sought understanding through observation of nature rather than textual study, and they were both based on cyclical patterns rather than linear progress [3].

The original Daoist classics (*Dao De Jing* and *Zhuangzi*) contain allusions to complementary forces but lack a systematic Yin-Yang cosmology. The *Dao De Jing* says:

"The Dao produces the One; the One produces the Two; the Two produce the Three; and the Three produce the ten thousand things. The ten thousand things carry the Yin and embrace the Yang, and through the blending of the Qi they achieve harmony" [1].

This passage acknowledges Yin-Yang but subordinates it to the Dao. As the traditions merged, Yin-Yang principles provided Daoism with a systematic cosmology; a comprehensive framework for understanding natural processes. It also provided medical theories along with principles for health maintenance and longevity [4].

Yin-Yang also provided an alchemical foundation for understanding transformation in both external and internal alchemy, with a ritual structure for organizing religious ceremonies, and meditative techniques for circulating energy within the body.

The *Taiqing* (太清, Supreme Clarity) and *Shangqing* (上清, Highest Clarity) Daoist schools, emerging in the 4th-5th centuries CE, represent the full integration of these traditions, with elaborate methods for manipulating Yin and Yang energies within the body through visualization, breath control, and ritual [5].

Medicine: The Harmonious Body

Perhaps no field demonstrates the practical application of Yin-Yang philosophy better than traditional Chinese medicine. The canonical text *Huangdi Neijing* (黃帝內經, The Yellow Emperor's Inner Classic), compiled between the 2nd century BCE and the 2nd century CE, established a medical system based entirely on the balance of Yin and Yang energies.

This medical system understands health as the dynamic balance of Yin and Yang, and illness as their imbalance or blockage. Diagnosis is made to determine the pattern of disharmony, and treatment is made to restore the proper balance.

The text states: "The human body is a small universe. The universe has day and night; the human body has activity and rest. The universe has four seasons; the human body has four limbs. All things in the universe correspond with something in the human body" [4].

Key therapeutic approaches include:

- Acupuncture: Manipulating the flow of Qi through meridians to balance Yin and Yang
- Herbology: Classifying herbs by their Yin or Yang properties
- Moxibustion: Applying heat to stimulate Yang energy
- Dietary therapy: Balancing foods according to their energetic properties
- Qigong: Movement and breathing exercises to regulate internal energies

Feng Shui

Feng Shui (風水, "wind and water"), the traditional Chinese practice of harmonizing individuals with their surroundings, represents another practical application of Yin-Yang philosophy. Originally called *Kanyu* (堪輿, "the way of Heaven and Earth"), this discipline evaluates how Qi flows through landscapes and buildings.

The practice involves balancing Yin spaces (rest, stillness, privacy) with Yang spaces (activity, brightness, socialization), arranging environments to create harmonious flow using the Five Phases to determine optimal positioning and relationships. It seeks to align human habitations with natural patterns and cosmic orientations.

The ancient Burial Book (葬書, *Zangshu*) attributed to Guo Pu (郭璞, 276-324 CE) states: "Qi rides the wind and scatters, but is retained when encountering water." This reflects the fundamental concern with how energy moves through environments and how humans can arrange their surroundings to benefit from balanced energies [3].

Internal Alchemy: The Transformation of Self

Internal alchemy (*neidan*, 內丹) represents perhaps the most sophisticated application of Yin-Yang philosophy to human development. Emerging from the Tang Dynasty (618-907 CE) and flourishing during the Song Dynasty (960-1279 CE), this tradition used Yin-Yang principles to create detailed maps of inner spiritual transformation.

Key texts like the *Wuzhen pian* (悟真篇, Awakening to Reality) by Zhang Boduan (張伯端, 987-1082) and the *Cantong qi* (參同契, The Seal of the Unity of the Three) describe processes of internal refinement using deliberately obscure alchemical language [5].

These texts refer to gathering and refining the Three Treasures: Jing (精, essence), Qi (氣, vital energy), and Shen (神, spirit), reversing the natural flow of energy ("contrary motion"), Uniting internal Yin and Yang to create the "immortal embryo", and transmutation of coarse energies into refined consciousness.

The practice was described as: "Taking Heaven as your cauldron, Earth as your furnace, Kan (water,   ) as your lead, and Li (fire,   ) as your mercury." These cryptic instructions used Yin-Yang symbolism from the *Yijing* to guide advanced meditation practices [7].

Beyond Natural Philosophy

While Yin-Yang theory began as a cosmological framework, it inevitably influenced Chinese thinking about society and governance. This application was neither simplistic nor oppressive—

rather, it emphasized complementarity, balance, and appropriate timing in social relationships.

The application of Yin-Yang principles to gender has often been misunderstood in the West as simply reinforcing patriarchy. The reality was more nuanced; the sexes were viewed as complementary rather than hierarchical. Classical texts emphasize the mutual necessity of masculine and feminine qualities. The Book of Changes states: "The interaction of one Yin and one Yang is called the Dao" [7].

Both men and women were understood to embody both Yin and Yang qualities in different contexts. The Huainanzi observes: "Fire that has reached its limit must return to water; Yang that has reached its limit must return to Yin." The forces were cyclical, and not static. The ideal was not absolute Yang dominance but harmonious interplay between Yin and Yang qualities in both society and individuals. Historical periods were seen as alternating between more Yin and more Yang styles of governance, with neither being permanently superior [3].

The classical phrase "men manage external affairs, women manage internal affairs" (男主外女主內) reflected a division of labor based on Yin-Yang principles, but did not necessarily imply value judgment. Indeed, the management of household affairs in traditional China conveyed significant power and responsibility.

A Harmonious Worldview

In political philosophy, Yin-Yang thinking has woven itself deeply into governance concepts across Chinese history. The cyclical theory of dynasties understood the rise and fall of ruling powers through the natural rhythm of Yin-Yang cycles. As recorded in the Book of Han (漢書), "When Yang reaches its extreme, Yin is born within it," explaining how even the mightiest dynasty carries the seeds of its eventual decline [2].

Effective governance embraced this cyclical understanding, recognizing that periods of active expansion (Yang) naturally give way to consolidation and conservation (Yin). The wisest rulers acknowledged these patterns and adapted their strategies accordingly. The ideal government combined both Yin qualities of receptivity, caution, and conservation with Yang qualities of decisiveness, innovation, and expansion to create a balanced bureaucracy that could weather changing circumstances [3].

Seasonal governance became another expression of this philosophy, with the Lüshi Chunqiu advising rulers to align their policies with the energy of each season: promoting growth in spring, encouraging development in summer, collecting and harvesting in autumn, and storing and conserving in winter [8].

During the Han Dynasty, the historian Dong Zhongshu systematized the application of Yin-Yang theory to governance in his work "Luxuriant Dew of the Spring and Autumn Annals," creating an integrated cosmological-political system that would influence Chinese governance for centuries to come [3].

Yin-Yang in Daily Life

While philosophical treatments of Yin-Yang theory were often the domain of educated elites, the concept permeated all levels of Chinese society, embedding itself in popular culture, folk religion, and daily practices. For ordinary people, Yin-Yang philosophy manifested in numerous aspects of life, structuring their understanding of the world and their place within it.

Festival observances followed the lunar calendar, which divided the year into Yin and Yang periods with celebrations marking transitions between them. The Winter Solstice (*Dongzhi*) celebrated the rebirth of Yang energy as days began to lengthen, while the Summer Solstice (*Xiazhi*) acknowledged the emergence of Yin within peak Yang as days would soon begin to shorten. Ancestral veneration practices recognized that ancestors inhabited the Yin realm while the living dwelled in the Yang realm, with proper rituals maintaining the beneficial connection between these two domains [3].

Folk medicine applied simple Yin-Yang classifications to foods, environments, and bodily conditions, informing everyday health practices from dietary choices to sleeping arrangements.. Traditional homes were arranged according to Yin-Yang principles, with the orientation of buildings, placement of ancestor shrines, and design of courtyards all reflecting cosmic patterns that connected human dwellings to universal forces. Agricultural communities followed planting, harvesting, and storage practices guided by cycles understood through Yin-Yang theory, as recorded in texts like the Monthly Ordinances [8].

The Almanac (*Tongshu*) became an essential household item throughout China, providing guidance for aligning daily activities with Yin-Yang cycles. Far from being esoteric knowledge, these principles structured the rhythms of ordinary life across Chinese society, creating a shared cosmological understanding that connected the humblest farmer to the grand patterns of the universe [3].

Artistic Expressions of Harmony

Yin-Yang philosophy profoundly shaped Chinese aesthetic sensibilities across all artistic domains. Landscape painting developed around the interplay of mountain (Yang) and water (Yin), embodying cosmic harmony through the balanced representation of these complementary elements. Poetry flourished through contrasting images and complementary couplets that reflected Yin-Yang balance in linguistic form.

Architecture evolved to create dynamic flow between enclosed (Yin) and open (Yang) areas, establishing spaces that mimicked the cosmic dance of opposing yet complementary forces. Musical theories of harmony and resonance were founded on Yin-Yang principles, creating compositions that moved between tension and resolution. Even calligraphy expressed Yin-Yang interdependence through the dynamic tension between the solid stroke and empty space, with each giving meaning and form to the other.

The 11th-century poet Su Dongpo captured this sensibility perfectly when he wrote, "The landscape has material form, yet reaches into the formless," expressing the sentiment that the perception that sees the interpenetration of opposite qualities as the very essence of beauty and meaning [3].

The emphasis on relationship, process, and mutual causality aligns remarkably well with modern complexity science and systems theory, providing age-old wisdom for today's complex problems. The recognition of natural balance and cyclic renewal offers profound insights for sustainable ecological thinking at a time when environmental harmony has never been more crucial.

Traditional Chinese medicine, based on Yin-Yang principles, has gained increasing recognition as a valuable complement to bio medicine, offering holistic approaches to health and healing. The concept of integrating opposing qualities within the psyche resonates with Jungian psychology and other approaches to mental wellness that seek wholeness rather than one-sided development. As a non-dualistic framework, Yin-Yang philosophy offers alternatives to Western either/or thinking that can enrich cross-cultural dialogue and understanding.

As global consciousness evolves beyond simple cultural dichotomies, Yin-Yang philosophy offers a model of difference that is neither relativistic nor absolutist. Its key contribution may be the insight that seeming opposites can be understood as mutually defining rather than mutually exclusive, dynamically transforming rather than statically opposed, contextually relative rather than universally fixed, and complementary rather than contradictory.

The contemporary philosopher François Jullien observes that "the Chinese conception of efficacy does not oppose thought and action, being and doing, theory and practice... Instead of constructing an ideal form that one then projects onto reality, the Chinese sage learns to detect the factors whose configuration is favorable to the task at hand" [10]. This practical wisdom, derived from Yin-Yang thinking, continues to offer valuable perspectives on harmonious action in a complex world.

As the Zhuangzi reminds us: "The ten thousand things are one. We call them by different names when they appear in different forms." Beneath the apparent dualities of existence, Yin-Yang philosophy perceives an underlying unity expressed through endless transformation—a vision that continues to enrich our understanding of both cosmos and consciousness.

Chapter 3: Endnotes

1. A. C. Graham, *Disputers of the Tao: Philosophical Argument in Ancient China* (La Salle, IL: Open Court, 1989).
2. Sima Qian. *Records of the Grand Historian*, trans. Burton Watson. New York: Columbia University Press, 1993.
3. Kohn, Livia. *The Daoist Tradition: An Introduction.* 2nd ed. Boulder: Shambhala Publications, 2020.
4. Nathan Sivin, *Medicine, Philosophy and Religion in Ancient China* (Aldershot: Variorum, 1995).
5. Isabelle Robinet, *Taoism: Growth of a Religion* (Stanford: Stanford University Press, 1997).
6. John S. Major, *The Huainanzi: A Guide to Ancient Chinese Cosmology* (Chicago: University of Chicago Press, 2015).
7. Richard Wilhelm, trans., *The I Ching: A Guide to Life Wisdom* (Princeton: Princeton University Press, 1967).
8. John Knoblock and Jeffrey Riegel, trans., *The Annals of Lü Buwei* (*Lüshi Chunqiu*) (Stanford: Stanford University Press, 2000).
9. W. Allyn Rickett, trans., *Guanzi: Political, Economic, and Philosophical Essays from Early China*, Vols. 1–2 (Princeton: Princeton University Press, 1985–1998).
10. François Jullien, *The Propensity of Things: Toward a History of Efficacy in China*, trans. Janet Lloyd (New York: Zone Books, 1995).

Chapter 4

The Arrival of Buddhism

Cultural Context of Transmission

The ancient routes of the Silk Road did more than carry silk, spices, and precious goods between East and West; they became channels for the transmission of ideas that would forever alter the spiritual landscape of China [1]. Along these dusty paths traveled not only merchants with their laden caravans but also monks with their sacred texts, bringing the Buddha's teachings from their Indian homeland into the Central Kingdom.

Early contact between China and Buddhism came in sporadic waves. Historical records mention the arrival of Buddhist monks as early as the 1st century BCE, though these initial encounters left little lasting impression. It wasn't until the Eastern Han Dynasty (25-220 CE) that Buddhism began to take root in Chinese soil. Emperor Ming of Han, according to later traditions, dreamed of a golden figure flying over his palace—an omen that prompted him to send emissaries westward in search of this radiant being. Whether historical fact or pious legend, this story marks a turning point in the narrative of Buddhism's eastward journey.

The true pioneers of Buddhism's transmission to China were the translators who undertook the monumental task of rendering Sanskrit texts into Chinese. Among the most significant was An Shigao, a Parthian prince who renounced his claim to the throne to become a Buddhist monk. Arriving in Luoyang around 148 CE, he established China's first translation bureau, producing Chinese versions of texts on meditation practices and basic Buddhist doctrine [2,3]. Not long after came Lokaksema, a Kushan monk who introduced *Mahayana sutras* to Chinese readers, including the influential *Pratyutpanna Samadhi Sutra* and the *Astasahasrika Prajnaparamita* (Perfection of Wisdom in 8,000 Lines) [2].

These early translators faced formidable challenges. Not only did they struggle with the vast linguistic differences between Sanskrit and Chinese, but they also encountered concepts that had no easy parallel in Chinese thought [4]. How could one express the complex Indian cosmology, with its multiple heavens and hells, in terms that would make sense to people raised in the pragmatic traditions of Confucianism and Daoism? How could the Sanskrit phonetics, so rich in consonant clusters, be rendered in a language built on monosyllabic characters?

Despite these hurdles, translation continued, generation after generation, eventually producing a Chinese Buddhist canon of staggering proportions. Yet Buddhism's reception in China was far from uniformly warm. Many viewed this foreign religion with suspicion. Court officials, steeped in Confucian tradition, criticized Buddhist monasticism as a threat to family structure and social order.

The Buddhist practice of celibacy seemed a direct affront to the cardinal virtue of filial piety—how could one fulfill one's duty to continue the family line while remaining unmarried? Moreover, the Buddhist tradition of monks begging for food appeared to encourage parasitic dependence rather than productive labor. Critics like Bao Jingyan accused Buddhism of being a foreign ideology that undermined the foundations of Chinese society [3].

Initial Points of Tension and Translation

The task of translation involved far more than finding word-for-word equivalents; it required building bridges between profoundly different worldviews. Translators struggled to find Chinese terms that could adequately convey Buddhist concepts. The Sanskrit word "*nirvāṇa*," denoting the ultimate goal of Buddhist practice—the extinction of suffering and the cycle of rebirth—was initially translated as "*wu*," meaning "nothingness" or "non-being." This choice inadvertently aligned Buddhist soteriology with the Daoist concept of returning to the primordial void, obscuring important distinctions between the traditions.

Similarly, the term "*Dharma*"—with its multiple meanings of cosmic law, truth, teaching, and phenomena—was often rendered as "*Dao*," a term already laden with meaning in Chinese philosophy. While this translation created an accessible entry point for Chinese readers, it also blurred the boundaries between Buddhist teachings and indigenous Chinese thought [4].

Perhaps the greatest point of tension lay in Buddhist monasticism's challenge to the Confucian social order. Confucianism placed supreme value on family relationships and hierarchical social structures. The monk who "left home" (*chu jia*) to join the *sangha* was, in a sense, abandoning these sacred duties. When a Chinese Buddhist shaved his head, donned the robes, and departed from family life, he was not just adopting a spiritual practice but committing a kind of social transgression. This tension would remain unresolved for centuries, with Buddhist apologetics repeatedly addressing the charge that Buddhism was fundamentally anti-familial [3].

The metaphysical frameworks of Buddhism and Chinese thought also created points of friction. Indian Buddhist philosophy, with its emphasis on emptiness (*śūnyatā*) and the illusory nature of the self, seemed at odds with the Chinese correlative cosmology based on the dynamic interplay of Yin-Yang and the Five Phases (*wu xing*). Where Buddhist thought emphasized transcendence from the cycle of *samsara*, Chinese cosmology sought harmony within the natural order. This fundamental difference in orientation would shape the development of Chinese Buddhism for centuries to come [4].

Adaptations and Syncretism

Faced with these challenges of translation and cultural acceptance, early Chinese Buddhists developed innovative strategies for making the *dharma* accessible. One such approach was *geyi* (格義), or "matching concepts," a method that deliberately explained Buddhist ideas using terminology from Daoism and Confucianism. This approach, pioneered by scholars like Zhi Dun in the 4th century, sought to build conceptual bridges between the unfamiliar Indian teachings and the familiar Chinese philosophical landscape.

Through *geyi*, Buddhist emptiness (*śūnyatā*) was compared to the Daoist concept of non-being (*wu*), while the Buddhist emphasis on compassion was linked to Confucian benevolence (*ren*). The Buddha's teaching of the Middle Way found resonance with the Confucian doctrine of the Mean. While later Buddhist scholars would criticize this approach as diluting the distinctive qualities of Buddhist thought, *geyi* served a crucial role in Buddhism's initial acceptance in China [3].

As Buddhism took root in Chinese soil, it began to develop distinctly Chinese characteristics. The *Mahayana* tradition, with its emphasis on universal salvation and the Bodhisattva ideal, found particularly fertile ground. Chinese Buddhism placed special emphasis on emptiness (*śūnyatā*) and compassion (*karuṇā*), two concepts that could be skillfully integrated with indigenous Chinese values. The *bodhisattva Avalokitesvara*, transformed into the female deity *Guanyin*, became perhaps the most beloved figure in Chinese Buddhism—a manifestation of compassion that resonated deeply with Chinese sensibilities [2,5].

The influence worked in both directions. Just as Buddhism was becoming Chinese, Chinese religious thought was being buddhicized. Daoist texts began to incorporate Buddhist elements, sometimes explicitly claiming that Laozi had traveled to India and taught Buddhism as an expedient means for the "barbarians" [4].

The *Laozi Huahu Jing* (老子化胡經, "Scripture of Laozi's Conversion of the Barbarians"), though later condemned as a forgery, represents this tendency to assert Daoism's primacy while simultaneously absorbing Buddhist concepts. Daoist longevity practices became infused with Buddhist meditation techniques, while Buddhist cosmology expanded to include Daoist deities [5].

Philosophical Parallels and Divergences

As Buddhism and Chinese thought engaged in this complex dance of mutual influence, certain philosophical parallels and divergences became increasingly apparent. The Daoist concept of *wu wei* (non-action or non-forcing) found a kindred spirit in Buddhist non-attachment. Both traditions valued release from desire and striving, though they framed this release in different terms. The Daoist sage achieved harmony with the Dao through naturalness and spontaneity, while the Buddhist practitioner sought freedom from suffering through the recognition of impermanence and non-self [3,4].

Yet these apparent similarities masked deeper differences. The Dao, as presented in the Daoist classics, was an ineffable yet generative principle—the mother of the ten thousand things. The Buddhist concept of *śūnyatā* (emptiness), though similarly resistant to direct verbal expression, pointed toward the absence of inherent existence rather than a mystical source of being. Where Daoism often sought longevity and harmony within the natural world, Buddhism aimed at achieving liberation from the cycle of birth and rebirth altogether [2,4].

The Buddhist doctrines of rebirth and karma posed particular challenges in a society deeply committed to ancestor reverence. Traditional Chinese ritual practices assumed a continuing relationship between the living and the dead, with deceased ancestors requiring offerings and maintaining influence over family fortunes. Buddhist rebirth, by contrast, suggested that the deceased would be reborn in new forms according to their karma, potentially breaking the continuity of family relationships that was central to Chinese social structure.

These tensions required creative negotiation. Over time, Chinese Buddhism developed hybrid funeral practices that honored both the Buddhist understanding of rebirth and the Chinese commitment to ancestral piety. Monasteries offered rituals to transfer merit to the deceased, helping them achieve better rebirths while maintaining the traditional focus on caring for ancestors [3].

The Sinification of Buddhism

Through centuries of adaptation and integration, Buddhism gradually became thoroughly Chinese. Far from remaining a foreign implant, it merged with indigenous traditions to create a religious synthesis that addressed core Chinese concerns with moral order, cosmic harmony, and causal relationships. The concept of karma was particularly important in this process, offering a cosmic principle of moral causality that resonated with traditional Chinese beliefs in Heaven's retribution [3].

The sinification process culminated in the emergence of distinctly Chinese schools of Buddhist thought. The *Tiantai* school, founded by Zhiyi in the 6th century, offered a comprehensive systematic philosophy based on the Lotus Sutra, incorporating Chinese preferences for harmony and integration. Its classification of Buddhist teachings into a coherent developmental scheme reflected the Chinese penchant for order and systematization.

The *Huayan* school, developing around the *Avatamsaka Sutra*, articulated a cosmic vision of mutual containment and interpenetration that resonated deeply with Chinese holistic thinking. In *Huayan* thought, each phenomenon contains and reflects every other, like the jewels in Indra's net that infinitely reflect one another—a vision of unity-in-diversity that harmonized with Chinese cosmological thinking [6].

Perhaps most successful in terms of popular appeal was the Pure Land tradition, which offered devotees the hope of rebirth in *Amitabha Buddha's* Western Paradise through the practice of *nianfo* (念佛), the recitation of the Buddha's name. This approach, emphasizing faith and devotion rather than philosophical sophistication or rigorous meditation, made Buddhist salvation accessible to ordinary people in ways that transformed Chinese religious life [2,5].

Besides the schools mentioned above, another school of buddhism would arise in the middle of the first millenium, combinining the principles of Dao and Buddhist Dharma. This school would leave a lasting impression on China and the world.

Chan Buddhism – Dao Meets Dharma

The autumn wind rustled through the reeds along the Yangtze as a strange figure appeared at the borders of the Liang Empire around

520 CE. Wrapped in a single robe despite the chill, with piercing eyes that seemed to look through rather than at those he encountered, this dark-bearded monk from India would later be known as Bodhidharma, the First Patriarch of Chan Buddhism. His arrival marks the beginning of a tradition that would become the most distinctively Chinese expression of Buddhist thought [2,5].

According to legend, Bodhidharma's first imperial audience ended in mutual incomprehension. When Emperor Wu of Liang proudly enumerated the temples he had built and the scriptures he had commissioned, seeking acknowledgment of the merit he had accumulated, Bodhidharma replied starkly: "No merit whatsoever." Confused and offended, the emperor asked who stood before him. "I don't know," came the reply. This exchange—whether historical or apocryphal—captures the essence of the Chan approach: direct, uncompromising, and resistant to conventional religious platitudes.

Bodhidharma then crossed the Yangtze River and secluded himself at Shaolin Temple, where he reportedly spent nine years in meditation facing a wall. This act of radical presence established a pattern that would define Chan practice: the prioritization of direct experience over intellectual understanding, embodied contemplation over textual mastery.

Though Chan would later become associated with a skepticism toward scriptures, the earliest Chan communities drew deeply from certain texts—particularly the Lankavatara Sutra with its emphasis on mind-only (*cittamatra*) teachings. This sutra's focus on the primacy of consciousness resonated with a Chinese intellectual tradition already sensitized to questions of mind through Daoist introspection. The sutra taught that all phenomena are projections of consciousness, and that enlightenment comes through recognizing the true nature of mind itself—a teaching that would become central to Chan's approach [5].

The early Chan practitioners were often mountain ascetics living far from the splendid temples and scholastic centers of the Tang Dynasty. They cultivated their practice in remote hermitages, embracing simplicity and direct contemplation. Masters like Daoxin and Hongren established small communities where work and meditation were integrated, anticipating Chan's later emphasis on the sacredness of ordinary activities. These communities existed somewhat at the margins of mainstream Buddhism, their practices deemed eccentric or radical by more conventional monasteries focused on sutra study and elaborate ritual [7].

Yet it was precisely this marginal position that allowed Chan to develop its distinctive character—a character deeply influenced by China's indigenous spiritual tradition, Daoism. In the remote mountains, far from imperial oversight, Buddhist practice could mingle freely with Daoist sensibilities, creating a spiritual approach that was simultaneously faithful to Indian dharma and deeply resonant with Chinese cultural patterns [4,5].

Daoist Influences on Early Chan

The fingerprints of Daoism are visible throughout early Chan Buddhism, though they appear not as explicit borrowings but as subtle colorations—a certain tone and temperament that distinguishes Chan from other Buddhist traditions. Perhaps most fundamental is the emphasis on naturalness (*ziran*) and spontaneity that flows from the Daoist classics into Chan practice.

When the Dao De Jing declares that "the Dao does nothing, yet nothing is left undone," it articulates a vision of effortless action that would find new expression in Chan's approach to meditation and everyday life [4]. The Chan practitioner, like the Daoist sage, strives paradoxically by not-striving, accomplishes by non-accomplishment. This approach reaches its clearest expression in the teachings attributed to Huineng, the Sixth Patriarch, who emphasized that true practice arises naturally from one's inherent Buddha-nature rather than from artificial techniques or graduated steps [5].

The Daoist concept of *wu wei* (non-action or non-interference) finds a Buddhist echo in Chan's emphasis on *wu xin* (no-mind or non-intentional practice). Both traditions recognize that the calculating, striving mind often creates the very obstacles it seeks to overcome. Just as the Daoist sage achieves harmony with the Dao not through willful effort but through receptive alignment, the Chan practitioner realizes Buddha-nature not by grasping for enlightenment but by letting go of the very notion of attainment.

Perhaps most significantly, Chan Buddhism inherited from Daoism a profound skepticism toward language and conceptual thinking. The opening words of the Dao De Jing—"The Dao that can be spoken is not the eternal Dao"—find their Chan equivalent in the famous declaration: "A special transmission outside the scriptures, not dependent on words and letters." [4,5] Both traditions recognize that ultimate reality transcends conceptual categories, that the map is not the territory, the finger not the moon it points toward.

This wariness of language did not mean a rejection of verbal teaching altogether—both Daoist and Chan masters were prolific writers and speakers—but rather a recognition of language's limitations and a deliberate use of words to point beyond themselves. The Chan master's shout or blow with a stick, like the Daoist sage's cryptic smile, communicates what discursive reasoning cannot [5].

Core Philosophical Tenets

At the heart of Chan philosophy lies a creative tension between two fundamental concepts: emptiness (*śūnyatā*) and Buddha-nature (*tathāgatagarbha*). From Mahayana Buddhism, Chan inherited the understanding that all phenomena are empty of independent existence, arising interdependently without fixed essence. Yet Chan equally emphasized that within this emptiness dwells the luminous potential for awakening—the Buddha-nature inherent in all beings [6].

This paradoxical unity of emptiness and Buddha-nature became the philosophical foundation for Chan's distinctive approach to practice. If Buddha-nature is already present, then enlightenment cannot be something to be achieved but rather something to be recognized. The barrier is not the absence of what we seek but our failure to see what is already here—like the proverbial fish who asks, "Where is the ocean?" [5].

This understanding sparked one of the great debates in Chan history: the question of sudden enlightenment (*dunwu*) versus gradual cultivation (*jianxiu*). The Northern School, descended from Shenxiu, emphasized gradual purification of the mind through disciplined practice, comparing the process to polishing a mirror until it shines. The Southern School, following Huineng, insisted that since Buddha-nature is already present, enlightenment must be sudden—not the culmination of a process but an immediate awakening to what has always been true [5,7].

This debate reflected deeper questions about the nature of practice itself. If enlightenment is sudden, what purpose does practice serve? Chan's answer was that practice is not a means to an end but the expression of enlightenment itself. The concept of "no-mind" (*wu xin*) captures this non-instrumental approach to meditation. In seated meditation (*zuo chan*, from which the Japanese term "Zen" derives), one sits not to achieve something but to embody the alert presence that is already Buddha-nature.

As Master Mazu expressed it: "Mind is Buddha; Buddha is mind." Ordinary consciousness, when freed from delusion and grasping, is itself the awakened state. The practitioner's task is not to transcend everyday mind but to see through the illusory distinctions that make it appear separate from Buddha-mind.

Iconoclastic Style and Literary Forms

Chan Buddhism developed distinctive literary and pedagogical forms that reflected its philosophical commitments. Perhaps most famous are the *gong'an* (better known by their Japanese name, *koan*)—enigmatic dialogues or situations that defy rational analysis. When a monk asks Zhaozhou whether a dog has Buddha-nature and receives the answer "*Wu*" (No)—despite the doctrinal insistence that all beings possess Buddha-nature—the contradiction creates a cognitive impasse that can only be resolved by breaking through conceptual thinking altogether [5].

These *gong'an* bear striking resemblance to the paradoxical anecdotes found in the Zhuangzi, with its conversations between sages and fools, its dream butterflies and talking trees. Both traditions use paradox not as intellectual puzzle but as existential challenge—a means of short-circuiting the discriminating mind to reveal a more direct way of knowing.

Chan poetry developed a distinctive voice, often using nature imagery to evoke the immediacy of awakened experience. When Chan master Wumen wrote, "Spring comes: grass grows by itself," he was expressing not just a seasonal observation but a profound insight into the self-sufficient unfolding of Buddha-nature. The imagery of mountains and rivers, clouds and moon that pervades Chan poetry owes much to the Daoist aesthetic sensibility, with its appreciation for the uncarved and unadorned [4].

Perhaps most characteristic of Chan teaching is its use of absurdity, humor, and direct physical gestures to break through conceptual fixation. When Master Gutei responds to every question by raising one finger, or when Yunmen answers his own question "What is Buddha?" with "Dried shit-stick," these shocking responses serve to derail the conceptualizing mind. The laughter that often accompanies Chan enlightenment stories signals not amusement but liberation—the sudden release from rigid patterns of thought into the spaciousness of direct experience [5].

The Sixth Patriarch and the Southern School

No figure looms larger in Chan history than Huineng, the Sixth Patriarch, whose life and teachings are recorded in the Platform Sutra—a text unique in being the only Chinese composition to be accorded the status of "sutra." Born to a poor family in the south, unable to read or write, Huineng represents the Chan insistence that true understanding transcends formal learning. According to tradition, he attained enlightenment upon hearing a single line from the Diamond Sutra: "Develop a mind that dwells nowhere."

The story of Huineng's dharma transmission embodies Chan's radical meritocracy. When the Fifth Patriarch Hongren sought a successor, his senior disciple Shenxiu composed a verse reflecting his understanding:

"The body is the Bodhi tree, The mind like a bright mirror stand. Time and again brush it clean, Let no dust alight."

Huineng, hearing this verse, responded with his own:

"Bodhi originally has no tree, The bright mirror has no stand. Fundamentally there is not a single thing, Where could dust alight?"

In this exchange, we see the crystallization of Chan's non-dual approach. Where Shenxiu's verse implies a separation between mind and defilement, practitioner and practice, Huineng's response dissolves these distinctions. There is no separate self to be purified, no dust foreign to the mirror—just the ever-present clarity of original mind.

The Platform Sutra abounds with metaphors that reveal Daoist influence. When Huineng compares the mind to space, which "contains the sun, moon, stars, pure land, kingdoms, mountains, rivers, and all things in the world," he echoes the Daoist vision of emptiness as generative void rather than mere nothingness. His teaching that "the mind ground is the essence" resonates with the Daoist emphasis on returning to the root.

Huineng's Southern School championed a radical non-duality that rejected all conceptual distinctions—even those between delusion and enlightenment, practice and realization. This approach finds a striking parallel in the Zhuangzi's famous butterfly dream, where Zhuang Zhou dreams he is a butterfly and upon waking cannot be certain whether he is Zhou who dreamed of being a butterfly or a butterfly now dreaming of being Zhou [4]. Both Zhuangzi and Huineng point to the constructed nature of the self and the arbitrariness of the boundaries we draw between states of being.

The Southern School's emphasis on direct insight over formal practice troubled more conventional Buddhists. Critics accused Chan of neglecting ethical discipline and systematic cultivation. Yet this charge misunderstands the nature of Chan's approach. By focusing on the awakened nature already present, Chan does not reject practice but reconceives it—not as a means to an end but as the natural expression of what we already are [5,6].

This integration of being and doing, insight and action, finds its fullest expression in the Chan arts—poetry, painting, tea ceremony, archery—where the most ordinary activities become vehicles for awakening. When the Chan practitioner sweeps the courtyard or drinks tea, these acts are not separate from meditation but are themselves the manifestation of Buddha-mind. In this seamless integration of the sacred and the everyday, we find perhaps the most perfect marriage of Daoist naturalness and Buddhist mindfulness [4,5].

As Chan Buddhism matured and eventually spread beyond China to Korea (as *Seon*) and Japan (as *Zen*), it carried with it this distinctive synthesis of Indian wisdom and Chinese sensibility. The Chan tradition represents not just the sinicization of Buddhism but a genuine cross-cultural dialogue in which both traditions were transformed. In Chan's emphasis on direct experience, its comfort with paradox, its celebration of the ordinary, and its artistic sensibility, we find a spiritual approach that transcends categories of "Buddhist" or "Daoist" to express a uniquely East Asian vision of awakening.

The story of Chan is ultimately not about the meeting of two static traditions but about the dynamic process of cultural integration itself—a process that continues today as these teachings find new expression in Western contexts. In studying Chan, we are not simply examining a historical tradition but participating in an ongoing conversation about the nature of mind, reality, and awakening—a conversation that, like the great doubt of a koan, remains perpetually unfinished [5].

By the Tang Dynasty (618-907 CE), Buddhism had become an integral part of Chinese civilization [2,5]. The foreign dharma had found expression in the native tongue, not merely linguistically but culturally and spiritually. The Buddhist sangha had established itself as one of the "Three Teachings" alongside Confucianism and Daoism, forming a tripartite religious complex that would define Chinese spiritual life for centuries to come. Though tensions and debates continued, Buddhism had successfully made the journey from foreign import to indigenous tradition, forever changing both itself and the cultural landscape it entered [3,5].

In this transformation, we find one of history's most remarkable examples of cross-cultural religious adaptation—a process that preserved the essential insights of Indian Buddhism while expressing them in forms resonant with Chinese sensibilities. The story of Buddhism's journey into China reminds us that religious traditions are not static entities but living realities that evolve through encounter and dialogue. What emerged was neither purely Indian nor purely Chinese, but something new: a Chinese Buddhism that would go on to influence all of East Asia and, eventually, the wider world.

Chapter 4: Endnotes

1. Sima Qian. *Records of the Grand Historian*, trans. Burton Watson. New York: Columbia University Press, 1993.
2. Heinrich Dumoulin, *Zen Buddhism: A History, Vol. 1: India and China* (New York: Macmillan, 1988).
3. Bryan W. Van Norden, *Introduction to Classical Chinese Philosophy* (Indianapolis: Hackett, 2011).
4. A. C. Graham, *Disputers of the Tao* (La Salle, IL: Open Court, 1989).
5. John McRae, *Seeing Through Zen: Encounter, Transformation, and Genealogy in Chinese Chan Buddhism* (Berkeley: University of California Press, 2003).
6. Paul Williams, *Mahāyāna Buddhism: The Doctrinal Foundations*, 2nd ed. (London: Routledge, 2009).
7. Morten Schlütter, *How Zen Became Zen: The Dispute over Enlightenment and the Formation of Chan Buddhism in Song-Dynasty China* (Honolulu: University of Hawai'i Press, 2008).

Chapter 5

Inner Alchemy and Martial Arts

Neidan: Inner Alchemy

Neidan, or internal alchemy, represents one of the most profound spiritual traditions to emerge from Chinese civilization. It developed as a direct response to the limitations of external alchemy (waidan), in which early Daoists sought immortality by ingesting potent substances like mercury, gold, and cinnabar [1]. After many alchemists met untimely ends through poisoning, Daoists turned inward, recognizing that the true path to immortality lay not in consuming external elixirs but in transforming one's own consciousness and energy.

In the tradition of Inner Alchemy, the human being is seen as a microcosmic reflection of the cosmos—a universe in miniature. To master oneself is to master the universe. Daoist inner alchemy builds on this insight to reverse entropy and transmute the mortal body into an immortal vessel of spirit. This perspective dissolves the boundary between self-cultivation and cosmic harmony [2].

The Three Treasures: Jing, Qi, Shen

Neidan is structured around the refinement of the Three Treasures (三寶), the fundamental substances that compose human existence:

Jing (精) – Essence (linked to reproductive fluids, vitality, stored in the kidneys). The most material of the three treasures, Jing is the foundation of physical life and reproductive potential. It is finite in quantity, and must be preserved and refined.

Qi (氣) – Energy (breath, life-force, circulating in the body's channels). The animating life-force or vital energy that permeates all existence, flowing through the cosmos and through every living being. It powers all biological processes, and is both material and immaterial.

Shen (神) – Spirit (awareness, consciousness, housed in the heart-mind). The most refined and subtle of the three treasures, it is connected to clarity of thought, spiritual insight, and transcendent awareness. It is the aspect of the self that is closest to the Dao.

The goal is to refine Jing into Qi, Qi into Shen, and Shen into Xu (虛, emptiness) or return to the Dao [2]. This process is referred to as the "Three Transformations" (三化). Through this alchemical process, the practitioner progressively refines grosser substances into more subtle ones, eventually transcending material limitation altogether. [3]

"The true fire does not burn, and the true water does not wet. Through stillness, the elixir is cultivated." — Daoist alchemical maxim

Core Practices of Inner Alchemy

Breathwork (Daoyin 導引, Tu Na 吐納)

Breath is Qi made visible and tangible—the most accessible form of vital energy.

Tu na (exhale–inhale) regulates and deepens breath to gather and circulate energy, drawing cosmic Qi into the body while expelling stale energy. Breath becomes the bridge between the gross body and subtle spirit, a tool for conscious intervention in normally unconscious processes. Advanced breathwork includes practices like "embryonic breathing" (*taixi* 胎息)—subtle, internal breathing reminiscent of a fetus in the womb.

Meditation (Zuòchán 坐禪 / Inner Visualization)

Stillness is the foundation (*jing* 靜). As the Daoist classic Nei Ye states: "When the four limbs are aligned and the blood and vital energy are tranquil, unify your mind and concentrate your will."

Meditation involves visualization of cosmic processes within the body: the microcosmic orbit, the Dan Tian, and the alchemy furnace (*ding*) where transmutation occurs [2,3]. Advanced practitioners move Qi through meridians, especially the *Ren* and *Du* channels (front and back midlines), in what is called the Microcosmic Orbit (*Xiao Zhou Tian* 小周天). Through meditation, the practitioner learns to direct awareness and energy to specific regions of the body, transforming physiology through focused intention.

Energy Circulation (Xing Qi 行氣)

This involves moving Qi through specific channels (meridians) using intention, breath, and sometimes subtle movement, with the objective of clearing blockages and harmonizing Yin and Yang aspects of one's energy body. Qi is gathered in the Lower Dan Tian (下丹田)—the elixir field just below the navel, considered the body's center of gravity and energy reservoir. More advanced systems include the Macrocosmic Orbit (Da Zhou Tian 大周天), connecting all major energy centers, and meridian fusion techniques that integrate the body's entire energetic system.

Energy Cultivation (Qigong 气功, "")

Qigong is a broader umbrella term that encompasses a wide range of practices including but extending beyond Xing Qi. Qigong involves comprehensive cultivation and refinement of qi, with the integration of breathing techniques, physical movements, and mental focus. It includes the application of qi for specific purposes (martial, medical, spiritual) combining varied methodologies and exercises.

In martial contexts, Xing Qi might be viewed as developing the "raw material" of internal energy, while Qigong represents the more sophisticated application and expression of that energy in movement and technique. Many traditional martial arts systems begin students with Xing Qi practices to establish a foundation before advancing to more complex Qigong methods that apply this energy in combative scenarios.

The slow, deliberate movements characteristic of Tai Chi function as moving Qigong practices. Principles like *song* (relaxation), *peng* (expansive energy), and *chan si jin* (silk-reeling force) all reflect Qigong's influence. The concept of "using *yi* (intention) to guide *qi*" manifests in applications where minimal physical effort produces significant external effect [3].

Dietary and Lifestyle Discipline

Inner alchemy provides recommendations for diet and lifestyle, such as abstention from heavy foods, meats, and intoxicants that deplete Jing or create energetic turbulence. Regular sleep, solitude, and connection to nature are considered important for aligning human rhythms with natural cycles.

Daoist monks often lived in mountains—reconnecting with Heaven and Earth, drawing inspiration and energy from these primal forces. The cultivation of virtue (*de* 德) was considered essential, as moral character was seen as inseparable from spiritual development [2].

The Golden Elixir and the Immortal Body

The "Golden Elixir" (金丹) is not a literal pill but a symbol for inner perfection—the convergence of spirit, breath, and essence into a single radiant point. Cultivating this elixir leads to:

Internal immortality: survival of consciousness beyond physical death, transcending the cycle of birth and death.
Spiritual rebirth: becoming a *Zhenren* (真人), a "True Person" who lives in harmony with the Dao and manifests its qualities of spontaneity, non-contention, and profound wisdom.

Some texts even suggest rejuvenation and bodily transcendence, producing "immortal bodies" (*yang shen* 陽神) that can exist independently of the physical form.

Daoist immortals (*xian* 仙) were depicted as sage-like beings who ride clouds, walk through walls, and commune with spirits—embodiments of freedom beyond ordinary human limitation [2].

Chinese Martial Arts

The mist hangs low over the mountains as a solitary figure moves through a series of flowing postures in a temple courtyard. Her movements appear deceptively gentle—a slow dance that masks the martial intent beneath. This is *taijiquan* (Tai Chi Chuan), perhaps the most famous expression of how Chinese philosophical and spiritual traditions transformed the art of combat into a path of profound self-cultivation. What appears to the uninitiated as merely physical exercise conceals layers of cosmological principles, energetic theory, and spiritual insight drawn from Daoism, traditional Chinese medicine, and Chan Buddhism.

The development of Chinese martial arts (*wǔshù*) represents one of the most remarkable integrations of philosophy and physical practice in human history. These arts evolved not merely as methods of self-defense but as comprehensive systems for understanding the relationship between body and mind, individual and cosmos, conflict and harmony. In their highest expressions, they became moving manifestations of China's most profound wisdom traditions [3].

Originated in ancient times, Chinese martial arts evolved through millennia before the emergence of Tai Chi Chuan. Archaeological evidence suggests combat systems dating back to the Xia, Shang, and Zhou dynasties (2000-256 BCE) [5], with military treatises like "The Art of War" demonstrating sophisticated martial thinking by the 5th century BCE [5]. Early martial practices focused primarily on battlefield effectiveness and weapons training rather than philosophical cultivation.

During the Han Dynasty (206 BCE-220 CE), systematic unarmed combat methods developed alongside weapons training. The Shaolin Temple, established around 495 CE, became a crucial center for martial arts development when military generals sought refuge there, bringing combat knowledge that merged with monastic discipline and Buddhist principles [4].

The Tang Dynasty (618-907 CE) saw martial arts flourish across social classes, with imperial military examinations establishing standardized combat systems. The Song Dynasty (960-1279) witnessed increased documentation of fighting techniques and the emergence of distinct civilian martial traditions emphasizing self-defense and personal cultivation alongside military applications.

By the Ming Dynasty (1368-1644), Chinese martial arts had diversified into hundreds of styles. It was in this rich martial environment that Tai Chi Chuan emerged, traditionally attributed to Chen Wangting in the 17th century during the Ming-Qing transition. Initially preserved within the Chen family, the art gained broader recognition when Yang Luchan learned and began teaching it publicly in the 19th century [5].

Unlike earlier martial systems focused primarily on combat efficacy, Tai Chi Chuan synthesized martial techniques with philosophical foundations from Taoism (yin-yang theory, wu-wei), Neo-Confucianism (ethical dimensions), and Buddhism (mindfulness practices) [3]. The martial tradition embodied Yin-Yang philosophy through movement.

The Chan Buddhist emphasis on embodied awareness particularly influenced Tai Chi's approach to "moving meditation," though the two traditions developed in different historical contexts and for different primary purposes [4].

This philosophical integration transformed Tai Chi Chuan from merely another fighting method into a comprehensive system for both martial application and personal cultivation, distinguishing it from many earlier *wushu* traditions [3].

Harmonizing with the Way of Nature

At the heart of Chinese martial arts lies the Dao, the ineffable source and pattern of all existence. To follow the Dao is to align oneself with natural patterns rather than struggling against them.

As the Dao De Jing expresses it: "The Dao follows what is natural" [1]. This principle became central to the development of internal martial arts (*nèijiā quán*), particularly Tai Chi Chuan.

When the martial artist embodies the Dao, combat transforms from a contest of opposing forces into a dance of complementary energies. Rather than meeting force with force—a strategy that favors the stronger combatant—the practitioner learns to sense the opponent's intention (*yì*), redirect their energy (*jìn*), and respond with natural timing that requires minimal exertion. This is the martial expression of *wú-wéi* (無為), action that arises spontaneously in accordance with nature [1,3].

The legendary Tai Chi Chuan master Yang Luchan, who brought the art from Chen village to Beijing in the 19th century, was said to neutralize attacks with such subtle movements that opponents felt as if they had fallen into empty space. When asked how he achieved such mastery, he reportedly answered: "I do not move—they move themselves." This response perfectly captures the Daoist principle of letting nature take its course rather than imposing one's will through force [5].

The influence of Daoist thought appears throughout the classical texts on martial arts. The "Tai Chi Chuan Classic," attributed to the semi-mythical figure Zhang Sanfeng, instructs practitioners to "use yi, not li" (use intention rather than brute force) and to "be still as a mountain, move like a great river." These poetic instructions point toward a profound truth: that effective martial skill emerges not from the accumulation of techniques but from the cultivation of natural principles.

This approach transforms combat training into a form of moving meditation. Each practice session becomes an opportunity to experience the Dao directly—not as an abstract concept but as an embodied reality. The practitioner learns to distinguish between movements that flow from the center and those that arise from peripheral tension, between actions that harmonize with natural mechanics and those that fight against them. Through years of refinement, these distinctions become increasingly subtle until the boundary between self and Dao dissolves.

The cultivation of Qi (Qigong) is essential in Chinese martial arts. According to traditional Chinese cosmology, qi flows through the human body along pathways called meridians, nourishing tissues and maintaining physiological functions. When qi flows smoothly and abundantly, health and vitality result; when it becomes blocked or depleted, illness and weakness follow.

Martial arts practices developed sophisticated methods for cultivating, storing, and directing this vital energy. These methods, collectively known as qigong (氣功, "energy work"), include breath control, focused attention, specific body alignments, and visualization techniques. Through these practices, martial artists learn to gather qi in the lower abdomen (the *dāntián*, or "elixir field"), direct it through the body's meridians, and express it through physical movements.

The deliberate cultivation of qi distinguishes internal martial arts from their external counterparts. While external styles (*wàijiā quán*) like Shaolin Kung Fu initially emphasize physical conditioning and technique, internal styles like *taijiquan*, *baguazhang*, and *xingyiquan* focus from the beginning on energy circulation and whole-body coordination. As Master Wu Yuxiang wrote in the 19th century: "The mind is the commander, the qi is the flag, and the body is the soldier" [3,5].

In practice, this means that before learning complex techniques, the internal martial artist must master fundamental energetic principles: rooting (connecting firmly to the ground), central equilibrium (maintaining the body's center of gravity), and silk-reeling (spiraling movements that integrate the whole body). These principles transform the body from a collection of disparate parts into a unified energetic system capable of receiving, neutralizing, and issuing force with remarkable efficiency.

The qigong methods embedded within martial arts serve both martial and health purposes. The same practices that develop "internal power" (*nèijìn*) for combat also nourish the organs, strengthen the immune system, and promote longevity. This dual purpose reflects the holistic nature of Chinese thinking, which never separated martial efficacy from broader concerns of health and spiritual development [3].

Many Tai Chi Chuan masters lived to remarkable old age while maintaining their martial abilities, demonstrating in their own bodies the life-nurturing aspects of their art. When the renowned master Cheng Man-ch'ing was asked in his later years about the greatest benefit of taijiquan, he replied not with tales of combat victories but with a simple observation: "I am in my seventies but have the health of a thirty-year-old" [5]. This integration of martial skill and health cultivation remains one of the most distinctive features of Chinese internal arts.

Yin-Yang: The Dance of Opposites

Perhaps no philosophical concept is more visible in Chinese martial arts than the theory of yin and yang—the complementary opposites that, in their dynamic interplay, generate the manifest world. In taijiquan, whose very name references this principle (*taiji*, 太極, refers to the "supreme ultimate" state from which yin and yang emerge), every movement embodies this cosmic dance of opposites.

The taijiquan practitioner learns to distinguish and transition smoothly between qualities: substantial and insubstantial, advancing and retreating, opening and closing, rising and sinking. Instructions such as "When the upper body is light and sensitive, that is yang; when the lower body is heavy and strong, that is yin." and "In each movement, there must be opening and closing." are expressions of a cosmological understanding that sees all phenomena as arising from the interplay of polar qualities.

In combat application, this philosophy manifests as the ability to adapt instantaneously to changing circumstances. When the opponent advances with force (*yang*), the practitioner yields (*yin*), only to counter at the moment when the opponent's energy wanes (becoming yin) with an explosive release of power (*yang*). This continuous modulation between complementary states creates a dynamic responsiveness that transcends fixed techniques [3].

Beyond yin and yang, Chinese martial arts also incorporate the Five Elements theory (*wǔxíng*, 五行)—wood, fire, earth, metal, and water—which describes how energy transforms from one state to another. In *xingyi quan*, one of the major internal arts alongside *taijiquan*, the core techniques directly express these elemental energies: the splitting fist embodies the cutting quality of metal, the crushing fist expresses the sinking nature of water, and so on [6].

These cosmological frameworks function as practical training methodologies. By embodying the qualities of yin and yang or expressing the transformative nature of the five elements, the martial artist develops a comprehensive understanding of energy dynamics that applies both in combat and in navigating life's challenges. As Master Sun Lutang, proficient in all three major internal arts, wrote: "The principles of taiji and the changes of yin and yang can be applied not only to boxing but to everything in the universe" [5].

The Still Center of Movement

While Daoism provided the cosmological foundations for Chinese martial arts, Chan Buddhism contributed essential insights into the nature of mind that transformed combat training into spiritual practice. The Chan emphasis on direct experience, present-moment awareness, and non-attachment offered martial artists a psychological framework that complemented Daoist energetic theories.

The influence of Chan is particularly evident in the mental training aspects of martial arts. Just as the Chan practitioner learns to observe thought without becoming entangled, the martial artist cultivates a "mirror-like mind" that reflects the opponent's movements without emotional reactivity. This quality of awareness, alert yet unperturbed, allows for spontaneous responses unclouded by fear, anger, or hesitation.

Many martial arts masters were also Chan practitioners who recognized the complementary nature of seated meditation and movement training. The legendary Shaolin Temple, birthplace of Chan Buddhism in China, became equally renowned for its martial arts tradition. This was no coincidence—both practices aimed at transcending the limitations of ordinary consciousness and revealing one's original nature.

The Chan concept of "no-mind" (*wúxīn*, 無心) found perfect expression in martial arts practice. No-mind does not mean unconsciousness but rather freedom from fixated thinking—a state where intention and action become one. The martial artist who achieves this state responds to attacks without the intervening steps of analysis and decision, acting with the spontaneity of a mirror reflecting images or an echo returning sound.

Master Takuan Soho, a Japanese Zen priest who instructed swordsmen in the 17th century, described this state in "The Unfettered Mind": "The mind must always be in the state of 'flowing,' for when it stops anywhere that means the flow is interrupted and it is this interruption that is harmful to the well-being of the mind." Though Japanese, his words capture a principle equally central to Chinese martial arts—the importance of maintaining a fluid awareness that doesn't become fixated on any single point [4].

The Chan influence also appears in the ethical dimensions of martial arts practice. The cultivation of non-violence (*ahimsa*) as a spiritual value transforms the purpose of combat training. Rather than learning to fight more effectively, the highest aim becomes transcending the need to fight at all. As the taijiquan master Cheng Man-ch'ing expressed it: "The highest level of taijiquan is using no technique to neutralize all techniques" [5].

This paradoxical approach—learning fighting skills to transcend fighting—reflects the Chan comfort with paradox as a teaching tool. Just as koans use contradictory statements to break through conceptual thinking, martial arts use the contradictions inherent in combat (seeking peace through fighting arts, cultivating softness to express power) to reveal deeper truths about the nature of conflict and harmony [4].

Tai Chi Chuan: The Supreme Ultimate Fist

Among Chinese martial arts, Tai Chi Chuan (*taijiquan*) represents perhaps the most complete integration of philosophical principles and combative movements. Developed during the late Ming and early Qing dynasties, it synthesized earlier martial systems with Daoist internal alchemy, traditional Chinese medicine, and Chan mindfulness practices to create an art that functions simultaneously as health practice, meditation in motion, and devastating martial system [3,5].

The origin of taijiquan is traditionally attributed to the Daoist sage Zhang Sanfeng, who allegedly created the art after observing a fight between a snake and a crane. Impressed by how the snake's yielding movements overcame the crane's direct attacks, he developed a martial system based on circular movement, yielding to overcome force, and the cultivation of internal energy. While historical evidence suggests a more complex lineage beginning with the Chen family in Henan province, this founding myth captures the Daoist inspiration behind the art.

In practice, taijiquan appears as a slow, flowing sequence of movements performed with precise alignment, coordinated breathing, and focused awareness. The practitioner learns to move from the center, maintain continuous circulation of energy, and express power through whole-body coordination rather than isolated muscular effort. These seemingly simple principles require years of refinement to master, leading to the saying: "Taijiquan is easy to learn but difficult to correct."

Beyond the solo form practice, taijiquan includes partner exercises known as *tuishou* ("pushing hands") that develop sensitivity to the opponent's energy, the ability to maintain one's center while disturbing the opponent's balance, and the skills of neutralizing and issuing force. These exercises provide a bridge between form practice and combat application, training the ability to apply philosophical principles under increasing levels of pressure [5].

The classical literature of taijiquan explicitly connects physical techniques with cosmological principles. The "Taijiquan Classic" states: "Taiji is born of *wuji* [the formless void before differentiation]. It is the mother of yin and yang. In movement, they separate; in stillness, they unite." This is not poetic flourish but practical instruction—the practitioner must physically embody these cosmic principles, experiencing how stillness gives birth to movement and how apparent opposites complement rather than conflict with each other [6].

The genius of taijiquan lies in its seamless integration of seemingly disparate elements: health cultivation and martial effectiveness, softness and power, structure and spontaneity. Through this integration, it offers a path of development that addresses the whole person—physical, energetic, mental, and spiritual. As one progresses in the art, these distinctions increasingly dissolve until, as Master Wang Zongyue wrote, "the entire body becomes a hand"—a unified field of awareness and capability [5].

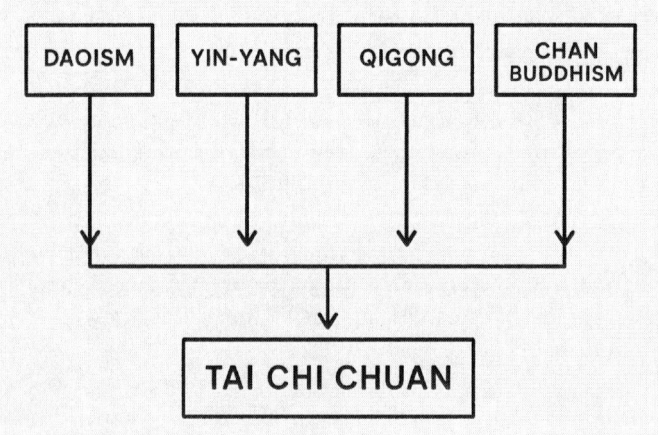

The Cultivation of the Sage-Warrior

The highest achievement in Chinese martial arts is not technical mastery but the cultivation of what might be called the "sage-warrior"—one who possesses both martial skill and spiritual wisdom. This ideal appears repeatedly in the martial classics, perhaps most famously in the opening of the "Taijiquan Classic": "In all the world, nothing surpasses the softness and weakness of water, yet in attacking the hard and strong, nothing can surpass it." This reference to chapter 78 of the Dao De Jing points to the paradoxical nature of true martial mastery—the discovery of extraordinary power through the cultivation of yielding softness [1,6].

The sage-warrior embodies several seemingly contradictory qualities. They possess devastating martial skill yet have no desire to demonstrate it; they can respond decisively to aggression yet maintain inner tranquility; they have transcended the distinctions between self and other that give rise to conflict in the first place. As chapter 68 of the Dao De Jing states: "The best warrior is not warlike" [1].

This ideal reflects a profound understanding of the true nature of conflict. Physical violence represents only the most obvious manifestation of discord—beneath it lie psychological tensions, social imbalances, and spiritual disconnections. The sage-warrior addresses conflict at its root rather than merely responding to its outward expressions. Through cultivating harmony within themselves, they naturally generate harmony in their surroundings.

The path to this integration involves the transformation of martial practice from external technique to internal realization. At the beginning stage, the student learns specific movements and applications—how to punch, kick, lock, or throw. At the intermediate stage, they study principles that transcend specific techniques—how energy flows, how balance is maintained and broken, how tension and relaxation alternate. At the advanced stage, they realize that these principles exist not just in combat but throughout nature—the same forces that govern martial interactions also govern the changing of seasons, the flow of rivers, and the movement of stars [3].

At the highest level, martial arts practice becomes indistinguishable from Daoist inner alchemy (*neidan*)—the transformation of coarse energies into refined spiritual essence. The martial classics describe this process using deliberately obscure language that parallels alchemical texts: "Store spirit in the bones," "Exchange the places of fire and water," "Return the elixir to repair the brain" [2]. These cryptic instructions point toward experiential realizations that cannot be conveyed through ordinary language.

Through this alchemical process, combat training transcends its original purpose and becomes a vehicle for spiritual liberation. The discipline required to master fighting techniques develops into the capacity to master oneself. The sensitivity cultivated to detect an opponent's intentions evolves into compassionate awareness of others' needs. The power developed to overcome adversaries transforms into the ability to overcome one's own limitations [2,3].

The Moving Dao in Contemporary Life

In today's world, the traditional martial arts of China continue to evolve and spread globally, though often in forms removed from their philosophical roots. Commercialization has sometimes reduced rich traditions to sport or exercise, stripping away the deeper layers of meaning that gave these arts their transformative power. Yet serious practitioners still approach these arts as comprehensive systems for human development—living traditions that offer wisdom particularly relevant to our fragmented modern existence.

The Daoist foundations of Chinese martial arts offer a corrective to the modern tendencies toward excessive specialization and disconnection from nature. In a culture that often separates body from mind, physical training from spiritual practice, and human beings from their environment, these arts demonstrate the possibility of integration—of finding wholeness in movement, wisdom in the body, and harmony with natural patterns.

The qigong practices embedded within martial traditions offer an experiential understanding of energy that complements mechanistic scientific models. Where conventional medicine often treats the body as a complex machine, qigong approaches it as an energy system connected to larger fields of influence. This perspective has proven valuable not only for health maintenance but for developing qualities of presence and centeredness essential for navigating life's challenges.

The yin-yang philosophy expressed through martial movement provides a model for navigating apparent contradictions without falling into either/or thinking. In a polarized society prone to ideological fixation, the martial artist's ability to flow between complementary states—to be both firm and yielding, structured and spontaneous, traditional and innovative—offers a living example of how opposites can complement rather than conflict with each other [3].

Perhaps most importantly, the Chan influence on martial arts reminds us that the ultimate battlefield is within [4]. The external conflicts we face—whether personal disagreements or global crises—often stem from internal disharmony. By cultivating peace within themselves, practitioners develop the capacity to generate peace in their surroundings. This does not mean passivity in the face of injustice but rather the ability to respond from centered awareness rather than reactive emotion [4].

The sage-warrior ideal embedded in Chinese martial traditions suggests a different kind of strength than that celebrated in much of contemporary culture. Rather than dominating others through force, true power lies in mastering oneself and responding appropriately to each situation. Rather than seeing conflict as a zero-sum game, the martial artist perceives it as an opportunity for creating new harmony. As Sun Lutang wrote: "The highest martial art is not to fight at all, but rather to persuade others not to fight" [5,6].

In their fullest expression, Chinese martial arts offer not just techniques for self-defense but a comprehensive path of personal cultivation—a way to transform one's entire being through mindful movement practices grounded in ancient wisdom. The outer form of punches and kicks conceals an inner science of energy cultivation; the apparent focus on combat masks a deeper concern with harmonizing opposing forces; the rigorous physical training serves as a vehicle for spiritual realization.

This integration of the physical and the philosophical, the martial and the meditative, represents one of China's most profound cultural achievements. In the flowing movements of taijiquan, the spiraling paths of baguazhang, or the direct expressions of xingyiquan, we witness philosophy made visible—the Dao not merely contemplated but embodied and expressed through the human form in motion. These arts remind us that the deepest wisdom is not found in abstract contemplation alone but in the lived experience of harmonizing body, mind, and spirit in accordance with natural principles.

Chapter 5: Endnotes

1. A. C. Graham, *Disputers of the Tao* (La Salle, IL: Open Court, 1989).
2. Robinet, Isabelle. *Taoism: Growth of a Religion.* Stanford: Stanford University Press, 1997.
3. Kohn, Livia. *The Daoist Tradition: An Introduction.* 2nd ed. Boulder: Shambhala Publications, 2020.
4. Heinrich Dumoulin, *Zen Buddhism: A History, Vol. 1: India and China* (New York: Macmillan, 1988).
5. Peter Lorge, *Chinese Martial Arts: From Antiquity to the Twenty-First Century* (Cambridge: Cambridge University Press, 2012).
6. Barbara Davis, *The Taijiquan Classics: An Annotated Translation* (Berkeley: North Atlantic Books, 2004).

Chapter 6

Zen: The Eastward Journey of Dao

The Transmission of Chan to Japan

When we trace the path of Daoist influence eastward across the sea to Japan, we find a fascinating story of cultural transmission, adaptation, and synthesis. The journey of what would become Zen Buddhism represents a profound example of philosophical cross-pollination, bringing Chinese Chan Buddhism into contact with Japan's indigenous spiritual landscape.

As we have seen, Daoism had a profound influence in shaping Chan Buddhism in China. Where traditional Buddhist schools emphasized scriptural study and doctrinal understanding, Chan (禪, Zen in Japanese) privileged direct experience and intuitive insight. It taught that all beings already possessed Buddha-nature and needed only to recognize it through meditation practice. During the Tang Dynasty (618-907 CE) Chan would go on to have a major impact on the indigenous culture and philosophy of Japan [1].

Long before Zen Buddhism formally arrived on Japanese shores, Daoist elements had been flowing into the archipelago through various channels of cultural exchange. During the Yamato period (4th-6th centuries), Japan eagerly imported aspects of Chinese civilization, including Daoist cosmology, astrology, medical theories, and calendar systems. These practical applications of Daoist thought quietly shaped Japanese understandings of time, space, and the body before any formal philosophical transmission.

The Tang Dynasty (618-907) marked another significant wave of influence, as Japanese monks, scholars, and envoys traveled to China and returned with immortality practices and spiritual cultivation techniques. These were rarely imported as pure Daoism, but rather blended with Buddhism and local animistic practices, creating syncretic approaches to spiritual development that prepared the ground for Zen's later arrival [2].

By the 9th century, Japan had embraced esoteric Buddhism through the Shingon and Tendai schools, established by Kūkai and Saichō respectively. These traditions already contained significant Daoist elements, particularly in their understanding of the cosmos and the subtle body [1,2]. Their practices of visualization, mantra recitation, and ritual gestures resembled aspects of Daoist internal alchemy (*neidan*), further familiarizing Japanese spiritual seekers with concepts that would later resonate with Zen teachings.

Indigenous Japanese Spirituality Before Zen

When Chan Buddhism arrived in Japan, it encountered a rich spiritual landscape already shaped by indigenous beliefs and previous waves of mainland influence. Understanding this existing cultural context is essential to appreciating how Zen would develop its distinctive Japanese character.

At the heart of Japan's native spirituality lay *Shintō*, meaning "way of the kami (spirits)." Unlike the more philosophical and systematic approach of Daoism, Shintō evolved as a complex of ritual practices and attitudes toward the sacred rather than as a formal doctrine. It expressed itself through shrine worship, purification rituals, and seasonal festivals that connected communities to their ancestral lands and deities.

The world of *Shintō* is filled with *kami*—divine presences that inhabit natural features, ancestors, and forces of nature. These are not abstract concepts but living realities that participate in human affairs and require proper acknowledgment. Mountains, waterfalls, ancient trees, and unusual rock formations are seen not merely as symbols of divinity but as actual dwellings of *kami*, worthy of reverence and ritual attention.

Central to *Shintō* practice is the concept of ritual purity, with elaborate cleansing practices and a careful distinction between the pure (*hare*) and impure (*kegare*). Unlike religions that locate the sacred in a transcendent realm beyond ordinary experience, Shintō finds it immanent within the natural world—a perspective that would later harmonize with Zen's emphasis on everyday awareness as the field of spiritual realization [3].

Even before Zen's arrival, however, Chinese influence had already carried Daoist currents into Japan. Daoist cosmology, seasonal rites, divination practices, and medical theories filtered into Japanese court and popular culture through waves of cultural exchange beginning in the early centuries CE. While often blended with Shintō ritual and Buddhist symbolism, these Daoist elements left a subtle but enduring mark: the sense of harmony with natural cycles, the attention to yin-yang balance, and the idea that human life participates in a wider cosmic rhythm [2].

While Shintō lacked a formalized cosmology like the sophisticated metaphysics of the Dao, its intuitive understanding of nature harmonized with the Daoist concept of non-duality. The Shintō practitioner, like the later Zen meditator, approached the world not as something to be explained conceptually but as something to be experienced directly and reverently [2,3].

The Dao's metaphysics of nature and *Shintō's* animistic reverence, would create a shared sensitivity that would later allow Zen's vision of non-duality to be received with unusual depth. By the time Zen arrived, Japanese culture had also been influenced by other Chinese traditions. Confucianism, brought through Chinese classics during the Asuka and Nara periods (6th-8th centuries), had profound influence on state administration, ethics, and education. Under figures like Prince Shōtoku, Confucian principles of hierarchical order, ritual propriety, and filial piety became intertwined with Japanese social structures [3].

Buddhism first reached Japan via Korean kingdoms around 552 CE, gradually establishing intellectual foundations through schools like Sanron (*Madhyamaka*) and Hossō (*Yogācāra*). These early Buddhist traditions introduced sophisticated philosophical concepts and scholastic methods that would provide the intellectual background against which Zen's more direct approach would later stand in contrast.

The 9th century saw the flourishing of esoteric Buddhism under Saichō (Tendai) and Kūkai (Shingon), who brought elaborate rituals, mandala visualizations, and cosmological systems from China. These esoteric practices, with their emphasis on the identity of the practitioner with cosmic Buddha-nature, created conceptual bridges that would later facilitate understanding of Zen's more stripped-down approach to the same fundamental insight [1].

Indigenous Wisdom: Resonances Across Cultures

The proto-Zen mysticism found in early Daoist traditions and Japan's Shintō shares striking resonances with other indigenous spiritual expressions around the world. These parallels deserve deeper exploration, as they reveal patterns in human spiritual experience that transcend geographic and cultural boundaries.

When we compare the mystical currents that preceded Zen Buddhism with the indigenous spiritual traditions of Australia and the Americas, we discover remarkable convergence of insight. These common currents seem to be evidence of a common spiritual understanding being formed from diverse human encounter with reality [4].

In Daoism, the Dao flows through all things as their generative principle—an unseen current animating the visible world. Similarly, Shintō perceives kami inhabiting mountains, rivers, and ancient trees—not as metaphors, but as actual presences with whom humans can enter into relationship [3].

This immediacy of the sacred in nature finds parallels in Aboriginal Australian dreamtime traditions, where the landscape is understood as physically shaped by ancestral beings whose presence remains active in specific sites. Native American traditions likewise approach natural features as living entities with whom humans have reciprocal relationships and ethical obligations.

What unites these diverse perspectives is a fundamental understanding that the sacred is not transcendent but immanent—not beyond the world but within it. For these traditions, the natural world is not a resource to be exploited but a community to which humans belong. Mountains, rivers, and forests are not merely settings for human activity but active participants in a cosmic conversation [4].

In Shintō, the graceful movements of the *kagura* dance, the offering of *sake* and rice, and the distinctive hand-clapping that awakens kami represent ways of harmonizing human communities with cosmic forces. Indigenous ceremonies worldwide—from Aboriginal *corroborees* to Native American sun dances—similarly serve not just as petitions to spiritual powers but as active participation in maintaining cosmic balance [3,5]. These rituals are not merely symbolic but actually effective in their practitioners' understanding, creating genuine connections between human, natural, and spiritual domains.

Many indigenous traditions similarly approach wisdom through story, silence, and observation rather than abstract conceptualization. Among the Lakota, for instance, silence is considered the language of the Great Spirit, and the most profound understandings are those that emerge from direct communion with natural forces through vision quest and ceremonial practice [4].

The Dao De Jing famously begins with the declaration that "the Dao that can be told is not the eternal Dao," establishing from the outset the ineffability of ultimate reality. Zen would later formalize this insight with its emphasis on "a special transmission outside the scriptures, not dependent on words and letters" [1].

Mountains are venerated as cosmic axes in Daoism (like *Wudang*), Shintō (Mount Fuji), and indigenous traditions worldwide—places where heaven and earth meet. Waters—rivers, lakes, and oceans—are understood as living entities and sources of purification across these spiritual systems. From Shintō shrines to Aboriginal sacred sites, spaces are never neutral but charged with spiritual significance, memory, and story [3,4]. To walk through the landscape is to move through layers of meaning, encountering presences that transcend the merely physical.

Finally, these traditions share a non-dualistic understanding of the relationship between material and spiritual realms. In the Daoist perspective, the material world is not separate from but an expression of the Dao; physical cultivation and spiritual development are inseparable aspects of the same process. Shintō similarly makes no clear distinction between natural and supernatural; the kami are both immanent within nature and transcend mere materiality [2,3]. For most indigenous traditions, what modern Westerners might call "supernatural" is simply a deeper dimension of the natural world, accessible through dreams, visions, and ceremonies [4].

These indigenous traditions would become mirrored in the teachings of Zen. When Zen teachers spoke of seeing one's true nature in the falling of leaves or the flowing of water, they were expressing an understanding that resonates with the oldest spiritual traditions on Earth: that the sacred is not elsewhere but here, not later but now, not in abstract concepts but in direct encounter with the world as it is [1].

Zen's Arrival in Japan: The Kamakura Period

The formal transmission of Zen to Japan occurred during a pivotal historical moment. The Heian aristocracy was in decline, and political power was shifting to the warrior class. This social transformation created receptive conditions for Zen's direct, unadorned approach to spirituality.

In the mist-shrouded mountains of medieval Japan, a spiritual revolution quietly took root. Eisai, a restless Tendai monk born in 1141, journeyed across treacherous seas to China, returning with seeds of enlightenment that would forever alter Japan's spiritual landscape. As the founder of Rinzai Zen, Eisai skillfully wove *Zazen* meditation practices with esoteric Tendai rituals, creating a uniquely Japanese approach to enlightenment.

His promotion of tea drinking—not merely as refreshment but as spiritual aid—would later blossom into one of Japan's most revered arts. When he penned *Kōzen Gokokuron* ("Zen for Protecting the Nation"), Eisai wasn't merely writing a treatise; he was offering

Japan's warrior class a spiritual compass that spoke to their need for discipline and directness. "Zen is not apart from the sacred teachings," he proclaimed. "It is the marrow of all the sutras."

A half-century later, another seeker named Dōgen, born in 1200, would walk a similar path to China but return with a profoundly different vision. After initial studies with Eisai, Dōgen found his true teacher in Caodong Chan master Tiantong Rujing. The Sōtō school he established upon his return rejected the very notion that practice and enlightenment were separate endeavors. While Rinzai approached awakening as a sudden breakthrough, Dōgen's Sōtō envisioned it as a gradual unfolding through the deceptively simple practice of "just sitting" (*shikan-taza*).

His masterwork *Shōbōgenzō* ("Treasury of the True Dharma Eye") revealed philosophical depths that would be plumbed for centuries to come. "To study the Buddha Way is to study the self," Dōgen taught. "To study the self is to forget the self. To forget the self is to be enlightened by all things." In these few words, he captured the essence of Zen's non-dual perspective—a wisdom that transcends the boundaries between subject and object, self and world.

As Zen took root in Japan during the Kamakura period, it found a natural ally in the rising warrior class. The samurai lived in a world defined by impermanence: loyalty tested by shifting allegiances, life suspended on the edge of a blade, death never far away. Zen's directness, its emphasis on clarity of mind and acceptance of transience, resonated deeply with this ethos.

Meditation became more than monastic practice—it was a warrior's discipline. The samurai who sat in *zazen* trained themselves to meet death without fear, cultivating *mushin* (無心), the state of "no-mind" where action flows without hesitation or self-consciousness. This psychological freedom proved as essential as skill with the sword.

Figures such as the swordsman Miyamoto Musashi and the Zen priest Takuan Sōhō exemplified this synthesis of martial art and contemplative practice. Their teachings reveal how swordsmanship could become a spiritual path: the stroke of the blade not merely a matter of technique, but an expression of presence, discipline, and harmony with circumstance [1].

Zen also shaped the broader cultural world of the samurai. The austere aesthetics of simplicity and impermanence—whether in the tea ceremony, the ink brush, or the architecture of temples and gardens—echoed both Shintō reverence for nature and Daoist spontaneity. In this convergence, the warrior class became unlikely custodians of a refined spiritual vision, carrying Zen beyond the monastery walls into the heart of Japanese culture [1,3].

The Dual Flowering: Rinzai and Sōtō Schools

As autumn gives way to winter only to birth spring anew, the two schools of Japanese Zen flourished through cycles of decline and renewal, each maintaining its distinctive character while sharing the fundamental commitment to *zazen* and direct experience.

The Rinzai school bloomed with particular vigor among Japan's warrior class and urban elite. Its emphasis on koan practice—those maddening paradoxical questions that defy rational solution—mirrored the samurai's need to transcend hesitation in battle. Masters like Enni Ben'en bridged spiritual worlds by integrating Zen with Pure Land practices, while Musō Soseki turned monastery gardens into living koans of stone and moss, all while whispering wisdom into the ears of shoguns. Centuries later, when Rinzai had grown dormant, Hakuin Ekaku breathed new life into the tradition through a systematized approach to koan training that continues to challenge practitioners today.

Meanwhile, the Sōtō school found fertile ground in Japan's countryside. Its emphasis on "just sitting" without striving for spectacular breakthrough moments resonated with the rhythm of agricultural life. Where Rinzai sought the lightning strike of sudden awakening, Sōtō trusted in the gentle rain of gradual cultivation. Its monastic communities became integral parts of rural life, and eventually, this less elitist approach allowed Sōtō to become the more widespread of the two schools, its teachings touching the lives of farmers and craftspeople far from imperial courts [1].

Zen's Cultural Impact in Japan

Like water seeping into soil, Zen penetrated Japanese culture so thoroughly that it became impossible to separate the two. No other imported tradition would be so completely transformed by—and transformative of—the Japanese spirit. Its aesthetic principles of simplicity, suggestion rather than statement, and finding beauty in imperfection infused nearly every Japanese art form.

In *sumi-e* painting, artists learned to capture essence through minimal brushstrokes, allowing empty space to speak as eloquently as ink. *Karesansui* gardens transformed raked sand and carefully placed stones into abstract landscapes where mountains could be conjured without a single tree being planted. Haiku poets discovered universes in dewdrops and falling leaves, embracing the momentary as a gateway to the eternal. Calligraphers transformed the act of writing into spiritual practice, each brushstroke revealing the writer's true nature more honestly than any confession.

Perhaps nowhere was Zen's influence more sublime than in the tea ceremony. What began as a monk's practical method for staying alert during meditation evolved through the hands of masters like Murata Jukō and Sen no Rikyū into a ritual where the simple act of preparing and serving tea became a profound exercise in mindfulness, humility, and presence. In the tea room's intimate confines, social distinctions dissolved, and participants could experience, if only briefly, the non-dual reality at Zen's heart.

For Japan's warrior class, Zen offered more than aesthetic principles—it provided a spiritual framework perfectly aligned with their precarious existence. Through *zazen*, samurai cultivated the mental clarity essential for battle. Zen's unflinching confrontation with mortality helped them face their own potential death with equanimity. The concept of "no-mind" (mushin) translated directly to combat, where hesitation meant defeat and spontaneous action meant survival. Even their aesthetic preferences—from the spare elegance of their living quarters to the unadorned beauty of their sword fittings—reflected Zen's minimalist influence.

The legendary sword master Miyamoto Musashi embodied this integration of Zen and martial prowess, while Zen monk Takuan Sōhō's writings illuminated the profound connection between the still mind of meditation and the fluid mind of swordsmanship. The way of the sword and the way of Zen became, for many, indistinguishable paths [1].

Rather than displacing Japan's indigenous Shintō tradition, Zen entered into a symbiotic relationship with it, like mountain and valley completing each other. Until their forced separation in the *Meiji* era, many sacred sites housed both Shintō shrines and Zen temples in harmonious coexistence. Zen's appreciation for natural simplicity complemented *Shintō's* veneration of nature, while distinctively Japanese aesthetic concepts like *wabi* (austere beauty), *sabi* (the patina of age), and *yūgen* (profound mystery) emerged from this spiritual cross-pollination [3].

Through this integration, a uniquely Japanese form of Zen emerged—more aestheticized than its Chinese parent, more attuned to nature's subtle voices, and more thoroughly integrated into secular culture. The resulting tradition wasn't merely transplanted Buddhism but something entirely new: a spiritual approach that would shape Japanese identity for centuries to come and eventually captivate seekers from around the world [1].

The Heart of Zen: A Philosophy of Direct Experience

At its philosophical core, Zen offers not another system of thought to master but a radical invitation to awaken—to see directly what has always been here. Like a finger pointing to the moon, Zen strips away elaborate spiritual scaffolding in favor of immediate encounter with reality itself.

The famous dictum often attributed to Bodhidharma, Zen's legendary founder, captures this revolutionary orientation: "A special transmission outside the scriptures; Not relying on words or letters; Pointing directly to the human mind; Seeing one's nature and becoming Buddha" [1]. In these spare lines lies Zen's fundamental challenge to conventional religious approaches. It draws simultaneously from the *Madhyamaka* tradition's sophisticated critique of language as inherently limited and the ancient Daoist suspicion of words as veils obscuring direct apprehension of the real [2].

Within this approach, Zen navigates what appears to be an irreconcilable paradox: all phenomena are empty of inherent, independent existence (*śūnyatā*), yet this very emptiness is the ground of potential awakening in all beings (Buddha-nature). Where lesser philosophies might strain to resolve this tension, Zen inhabits it comfortably, like a bird resting in thin air. As Dōgen expressed with characteristic directness, practice and realization are not sequential stages but simultaneous realities—we are already Buddha, but must realize this through dedicated practice.

Unlike traditions that view meditation as merely a means to an end, Zen places *zazen* at its very heart. The Rinzai approach uses meditation as stable ground for the lightning strike of koan investigation, while Sōtō considers "just sitting" not as technique for attaining Buddha-nature but as its very expression. "*Zazen* is not meditation to become a Buddha," Dōgen insisted. "*Zazen* is the expression of the Buddha-nature itself." In this light, each moment on the cushion becomes not preparation for enlightenment but enlightenment itself unfolding.

Perhaps Zen's most revolutionary aspect—the jewel hidden in plain sight—is its location of awakening within ordinary experience. Enlightenment is not an escape from the world but seeing it clearly as it is; the sacred is found not in special states but in chopping wood and carrying water; the extraordinary manifests through the ordinary. This profound insight found expression in the arts of daily life—tea ceremony, garden tending, archery, calligraphy—all approached not as mere pastimes but as spiritual disciplines where the infinite could be glimpsed through the finite [1].

From Mountain Monasteries to the Modern World

As Japan emerged from feudal isolation into modernity during the

Meiji era (1868-1912), Zen faced unprecedented challenges. State-sponsored secularization weakened traditional Buddhist institutions, yet paradoxically created conditions for Zen's transmission beyond Japan's shores. [1] What began as a tradition passed from master to disciple in remote mountain temples would soon touch minds around the world.

D.T. Suzuki, born in 1870 as Japan was reinventing itself, would become Zen's most influential ambassador to the West. Both scholar and practitioner, he presented Zen not as exotic Oriental mysticism but as a universal experience transcending cultural boundaries. Through countless books, lectures, and conversations, Suzuki's articulation of Zen influenced Western luminaries from psychologist Carl Jung to philosopher Martin Heidegger and popularizer Alan Watts. Though later scholars would critique his presentation as selectively modernized, Suzuki undeniably built the first substantial bridge connecting Zen to Western intellectual life.

Where D.T. Suzuki spoke primarily to scholars and intellectuals, Shunryu Suzuki (no relation) embodied Zen's practical wisdom for ordinary seekers. Arriving in San Francisco in 1959, this unassuming Japanese priest founded the San Francisco Zen Center and authored the modern classic Zen Mind, Beginner's Mind. His gentle insistence that "in the beginner's mind there are many possibilities, in the expert's there are few" offered a perfect entry point for Westerners overwhelmed by expertise yet hungry for authentic spiritual practice. Through his emphasis on humility and everyday mindfulness, Shunryu Suzuki transplanted not just Zen techniques but its living spirit into American soil.

Other remarkable teachers—Hakuun Yasutani with his rigorous koan approach, Taizan Maezumi integrating multiple lineages, Korean master Seung Sahn with his penetrating question "What are you?"—established Zen centers throughout Europe and the Americas. Each adapted traditional practices to modern Western life without diluting their essential power. Their efforts transformed what might have remained an exotic import into a living tradition now spanning continents [5].

Today, Zen has become a global phenomenon practiced in contexts its ancient masters could scarcely have imagined. Traditional monasteries in Japan and internationally maintain rigorous training schedules with their predawn meditation periods and mindful work practice. Urban Zen centers offer meditation instruction and community practice for lay practitioners balancing spiritual cultivation with career and family. Zen-influenced mindfulness practices have entered therapeutic settings and wellness programs, while Zen principles find application in leadership training, artistic endeavors, and approaches to daily life. What began as an esoteric monastic tradition now offers its wisdom in forms accessible to people of diverse backgrounds and circumstances.

The Enduring Appeal: Zen's Remarkable Resilience

What explains Zen's remarkable ability to thrive across cultures and centuries? How has a tradition rooted in medieval Chinese and Japanese monasticism come to speak so powerfully to contemporary minds? Several qualities contribute to its surprising resilience.

In a world drowning in complexity, Zen offers a refreshing simplicity. There are no elaborate theological systems to master, no hierarchies of deities requiring propitiation, no complex cosmologies demanding intellectual assent. Instead, Zen emphasizes direct experience rather than belief, practice rather than doctrine. "What is the Buddha?" asked a monk. "Three pounds of flax," replied his teacher—cutting through abstraction to the concrete reality before them. This directness continues to attract those weary of spiritual complications.

While many traditions strive to resolve paradox through ever more intricate explanations, Zen embraces mystery. Its koans deliberately defy logical solution, inviting practitioners to leap beyond habitual thinking. The simultaneous truth of universal emptiness and universal Buddha-nature remains not a problem to solve but a reality to experience. The unity of practice and realization—that we are simultaneously complete as we are yet in need of cultivation—reflects a comfort with apparent contradiction increasingly valued in a world where simplistic certainties crumble daily.

Unlike paths that separate contemplation from worldly engagement, Zen offers their seamless integration. Meditation provides a foundation not for escape but for engaged living; mindfulness extends beyond the cushion to infuse each activity; the sacred reveals itself in washing dishes as surely as in formal ritual. This integration speaks powerfully to contemporary seekers unwilling to divide life into spiritual and mundane compartments.

While maintaining its depths, Zen offers practices remarkably accessible to anyone willing to engage them. Seated meditation requires no special equipment beyond a cushion, no elaborate initiations, no particular beliefs. Direct perception—the simple act of being present to what is—remains available to all human beings regardless of background. This universality allows Zen practice to be adapted to various life circumstances without losing its essential character [1].

Conclusion: Zen as a Way of Being

Ultimately, Zen represents not merely a set of techniques or beliefs but a way of being: fully present to each moment, undivided between self and world, responsive rather than reactive, accepting impermanence as the nature of reality. The remarkable journey that brought Daoist-influenced Chan from China to Japan—where it encountered and harmonized with indigenous Shintō sensibilities—produced a spiritual approach simultaneously ancient and contemporary, culturally rooted yet universally accessible [2].

Through its emphasis on direct experience, non-duality, and the sacredness of ordinary life, Zen continues to offer wisdom to a world often fragmented, distracted, and alienated from immediate experience. Whether practiced in traditional monastic settings or adapted to contemporary urban life, its fundamental insights remain potent medicine for modern ills [1].

An old Zen saying reminds us: "The Way is not in the sky; the Way is in the heart." This insight—that awakening is not found in distant realms but in the immediate experience of this very moment—remains Zen's enduring gift. In a world perpetually seeking elsewhere, Zen gently, persistently points to the treasure we already carry, inviting us to wake up to the life that's always been right here.

Chapter 6: Endnotes

1. Heinrich Dumoulin, *Zen Buddhism: A History, Vol. 1: India and China* (New York: Macmillan, 1988).
2. Kohn, Livia. *The Daoist Tradition: An Introduction.* 2nd ed. Boulder: Shambhala Publications, 2020.
3. James H. Foard, *The Power of the Kami: Shinto and the Japanese Experience of the Sacred* (Cambridge: Harvard University Press, 1991).
4. Graham Harvey, *Animism: Respecting the Living World*, 2nd ed. (New York: Columbia University Press, 2017).
5. Morten Schlütter, *How Zen Became Zen: The Dispute over Enlightenment and the Formation of Chan Buddhism in Song-Dynasty China* (Honolulu: University of Hawai'i Press, 2008).

Chapter 7

Epilogue: The Way Beyond Words

In the beginning of the *Dao De Jing*, Laozi offers what may be the most honest first line of any spiritual text: "The Dao that can be spoken is not the eternal Dao." With this paradoxical admission—using words to declare the inadequacy of words—he invites us into the central mystery that has animated both Daoism and Zen across the centuries. We have journeyed through traditions that, at their heart, insist on their own inexpressibility. And yet, here we are, having filled pages with words about that which supposedly transcends language. What are we to make of this apparent contradiction?

Perhaps the resolution lies in understanding that words, in these traditions, function not as containers of truth but as indicators toward the truth. When the Sixth Patriarch Huineng tore up the Diamond Sutra, he wasn't rejecting wisdom but demonstrating that true insight cannot be trapped between covers. When Dōgen filled thousands of pages with his dense, poetic explorations, he wasn't contradicting Zen's supposed silence but using language to exhaust language, pushing words to their breaking point until the reader might fall through into direct experience.

The Unnamable Source

Both Daoism and Zen circle around an identical intuition: that beneath our conceptual understanding of reality lies something immediate, vital, and completely ordinary that cannot be captured in the net of language. The Daoist sages called it Dao—the Way, the flowing principle, the uncarved block—while carefully reminding us that any name distorts its essence. Zen masters pointed to Buddha-nature or Original Face, while using every trick of language to prevent their students from turning these pointers into concepts.

"Not establishing words and letters" stands as one of Bodhidharma's four foundations of Zen, yet this dictum comes to us, ironically, through words. Zhuangzi's tales delight in mocking scholarly disputation while themselves displaying literary brilliance. This apparent hypocrisy reveals a sophisticated understanding of language's paradoxical nature—it is simultaneously our most powerful tool for communication and the subtlest barrier to direct experience.

Consider how these masters approached the inexpressible:

Laozi offered poetic paradoxes: "The Dao is empty, yet inexhaustible." "The great square has no corners." "The best traveler leaves no tracks." Each statement undermines our conceptual categories, creating cognitive openings where direct intuition might arise.

Zhuangzi employed fantastical narratives and dialogue, using stories of talking animals and transforming sages to dissolve the boundaries of conventional thinking. His butterfly dream—"Am I a man dreaming I am a butterfly, or a butterfly dreaming I am a man?"—serves not as philosophical position but as dissolution of positions altogether.

Huineng, the illiterate woodcutter who became the Sixth Patriarch of Zen, demonstrated wisdom beyond words when he spontaneously responded to a verse about mind-dusting with his famous lines: "Bodhi originally has no tree, the bright mirror has no stand. Fundamentally there is not a single thing—where could dust alight?" His insight cut through conceptual understanding to direct perception of emptiness.

Dōgen, centuries later, would twist language upon itself in his masterwork *Shōbōgenzō*, writing, "To study the Buddha Way is to study the self. To study the self is to forget the self. To forget the self is to be enlightened by all things." Here, language serves not to explain but to create a kind of productive confusion that might crack open habitual patterns of thought.

What unites these seemingly different approaches is their shared understanding that the ultimate cannot be contained by concepts but must be directly experienced. Like scientists approaching the quantum realm, they discovered that ordinary language fails before the fundamental nature of reality. Their solution was not to abandon communication but to transform it—using words not as containers of truth but as catalysts for insight.

The Living Practice

If words ultimately fail, what remains? For both traditions, the answer lies in embodied practice—the cultivation of a way of being that aligns with reality as it is, not as we conceptualize it.

In Daoism, this practice centers on cultivating stillness and spontaneity. The sage empties himself of fixed notions, returning to the state of the uncarved block (*pu*) to act in accordance with nature's flow. As the *Daodejing* advises: "Do that which consists in taking no action, and order will prevail." This *wu-wei* (non-action) represents not passivity but action so attuned to circumstances that it appears effortless—like water flowing downhill, finding the path of least resistance yet eventually wearing away stone.

Zen's approach manifests most essentially in *zazen*—"just sitting." Not meditation to gain enlightenment, but enlightenment itself expressing through the simple act of sitting. As Dōgen insisted, practice and realization are not sequential but simultaneous. We do not sit to become Buddha; sitting is Buddha-nature manifesting. The practitioner cultivates what Shunryu Suzuki called "beginner's mind"—a state of openness, curiosity, and lack of preconceptions [1]. "In the beginner's mind there are many possibilities," he taught, "in the expert's there are few."

Both traditions emphasize seeing the world as it is, before the overlay of conceptual thought. Zhuangzi's story of Cook Ding, who butchered oxen with such perfect attunement that his knife never dulled, illustrates this principle. "What I care about is the Way," the cook explains, describing how he moves through spaces where there is room to move—perceiving reality directly rather than through concepts. Similarly, Zen master Seung Sahn would challenge students with the direct question: "What is this?"—not seeking a conceptual answer but an immediate pointing to experience before naming [2].

The practices of these traditions aim at nothing less than a fundamental shift in perception—from seeing the world through the filter of concepts to direct encounter with reality. The stillness of Daoist meditation and the alert presence of Zen *zazen* serve the same function: clearing away habitual patterns of thought to reveal what has always been present.

This is not a rejection of thought but a liberation from its tyranny. As the contemporary Zen teacher Norman Fischer observes, "Zen doesn't say there's something wrong with thinking. It just points out that thinking is just thinking" [3]. When we recognize thoughts as thoughts rather than as reality itself, we gain freedom to engage with life more directly.

The Paradox of Seeking

Here we encounter the central paradox that animates both traditions: how does one seek that which can never be found through seeking? If Buddha-nature is already present, why practice? If the Dao is our original condition, why cultivate it?

Daoist and Zen masters recognized this contradiction and incorporated it into their teaching. "The Dao that can be sought is not the constant Dao," warns Laozi, while Zen master Linji (Rinzai) taught, "If you meet the Buddha on the road, kill him"—a shocking instruction meant to prevent students from objectifying enlightenment.

This paradox finds perhaps its clearest expression in the Ten Ox-Herding Pictures of Zen, which depict the stages of practice through the metaphor of a herder seeking, finding, and taming an ox (representing Buddha-nature). In the final images, both ox and herder disappear, and the seeker returns to the marketplace with "bliss-bestowing hands"—utterly ordinary yet fundamentally transformed. The seeking was necessary precisely to discover that there was nothing to seek.

Modern cognitive science offers an interesting perspective on this paradox. What these traditions may be describing is not the acquisition of something new but the falling away of habitual patterns of perception and cognition that obscure our direct experience. The effort of practice eventually dissolves the very self making the effort, revealing what Japanese Zen calls "ordinary mind" (*byōjōshin*)—the natural state we've never actually left.

Why does this matter? In a world increasingly mediated through screens and abstractions, where virtual experiences replace direct ones, and where conceptual understanding is privileged over embodied knowing, these ancient traditions offer essential medicine. They remind us that life is not primarily a problem to be solved but a reality to be experienced. They suggest that our sophisticated conceptual frameworks, for all their utility, may actually distance us from the vibrant immediacy of existence.

The environmental philosopher David Abram observes that indigenous cultures maintained intimate relationships with the more-than-human world precisely because they experienced it directly rather than through abstract concepts [4]. Perhaps the Daoist reverence for nature and the Zen appreciation of ordinary moments offer similar wisdom—a return to direct participation in the world that might heal our modern alienation.

The Living Paradox

As we conclude this exploration, we return to the paradox with which we began: using words to point beyond words. Perhaps this contradiction is not a problem to solve but a koan to live—a productive tension that keeps us honest about the limitations of our understanding while continuing to communicate our insights.

The thirteenth-century Japanese Zen master Dōgen wrote, "To express the Way with the whole body and mind, hearing it with the whole body and mind, is like a dragon finding water or a tiger taking to the mountains." This vivid image suggests that authentic understanding is not abstract but fully embodied—a complete resonance between being and environment.

Both Daoism and Zen continue to offer this possibility: not escape from the world but complete immersion in it; not transcendence of ordinary life but discovery of its extraordinary depth. They invite us into a way of being that is simultaneously ancient and urgently contemporary—a way beyond words yet expressed through every gesture.

An old Zen saying reminds us: "Before enlightenment, chop wood, carry water. After enlightenment, chop wood, carry water." The activities remain the same; what changes is the quality of presence we bring to them. In this simple wisdom lies perhaps the most profound teaching these traditions offer—that the sacred is not elsewhere but here, not later but now, not in special experiences but in this very breath.

The ineffable Way continues, beyond all our attempts to capture it in words, flowing like water, empty like a valley, ordinary as dust, luminous as dawn. We honor it best not by conclusive statements but by the question that opens rather than closes: what is this?

Chapter 7: Endnotes

1. Shunryu Suzuki, *Zen Mind, Beginner's Mind* (Boston: Shambhala Publications, 2006).
2. Seung Sahn, *Dropping Ashes on the Buddha: The Teachings of Zen Master Seung Sahn* (New York: Grove Press, 1976).
3. Norman Fischer, *Training in Compassion: Zen Teachings on the Practice of Lojong* (Boston: Shambhala Publications, 2013).
4. David Abram, *The Spell of the Sensuous: Perception and Language in a More-Than-Human World* (New York: Vintage Books, 1997).

Manufactured by Amazon.ca
Acheson, AB